"Functioning as a biblical barist⸱⸱⸱⸱⸱⸱⸱⸱⸱⸱⸱⸱⸱⸱⸱⸱⸱⸱⸱⸱⸱⸱ the necessary theological tools to stud⸱⸱⸱⸱⸱⸱⸱⸱⸱⸱⸱⸱⸱⸱⸱⸱⸱⸱⸱ury eyes. For those tired of the faith⸱⸱⸱⸱⸱⸱⸱⸱⸱⸱⸱⸱⸱⸱⸱⸱ s a much-needed respite, a biblical o⸱⸱⸱⸱⸱⸱⸱⸱⸱⸱⸱⸱⸱⸱⸱ :an explore a different perspective on contemporary global issues."

—BECKY GARRISON, author of *The New Atheist Crusaders and Their Unholy Grail* and *Rising from the Ashes*

"Like a jolt of java, this book awakens the reader to the discipline of cultural context. Here is a non-bookish book on how all theology should be drenched in the smells and flavors of the house roast."

—LEONARD SWEET, PhD, professor, Drew Theological School, George Fox University

"Ed Cyzewski has provided an engaging and conversational introduction to theology in the contemporary setting that is attuned to the mission of God and sensitive to the contexts that shape our reflections on the Bible and Christian faith. In so doing he reminds us that good theology must always be lived out with others in the midst of everyday life as a witness to the gospel of Jesus Christ. This is a book for anyone interested in the relationship of theology to Christian faith and life in the world."

—JOHN FRANKE, professor of theology, Biblical Seminary

"*Coffeehouse Theology* provides a wonderful portal into the world of theology for those who want to think harder about their faith in postmodern times. With his disarming conversational style, Ed Cyzewski weaves a rich tapestry of meditations on God and everyday life, inviting us to take new angles of entry into timeless biblical truths. Ed shows us why good theology demands constant cultural dialogue."

—JIM SPEIGEL, of *Gum, Geckos, and God*

"In a world exploding with new ideas, new information, and new possibilities, we are all theologians—people seeking to understand the nature of our creator and the purpose of our lives in the here and now. In a culture rapidly shifting in consciousness, it is vital that we learn to read Scripture and the stories of our own lives with careful intelligence, humility, and a sense of wonder and adventure. In *Coffeehouse Theology*, Ed Cyzewski skillfully introduces readers to the important yet often misunderstood discipline of contextual theology and equips us to take our next steps toward making a life in the way of Jesus."

—MARK SCANDRETTE, author of *Soul Graffiti* and *Making a Life in the Way of Jesus*

ED CYZEWSKI

NAVPRESS

NAVPRESS⬤

NavPress is the publishing ministry of The Navigators, an international Christian organization and leader in personal spiritual development. NavPress is committed to helping people grow spiritually and enjoy lives of meaning and hope through personal and group resources that are biblically rooted, culturally relevant, and highly practical.

For a free catalog go to www.NavPress.com
or call 1.800.366.7788 in the United States or 1.800.839.4769 in Canada.

© 2008 Ed Cyzewski

All rights reserved. No part of this publication may be reproduced in any form without written permission from NavPress, P.O. Box 35001, Colorado Springs, CO 80935. www.navpress.com

NAVPRESS and the NAVPRESS logo are registered trademarks of NavPress. Absence of ® in connection with marks of NavPress or other parties does not indicate an absence of registration of those marks.

ISBN-13: 978-1-60006-277-3

Cover design by studiogearbox
Cover photo by Veer

Published in association with the literary agency of Sanford Communications, Portland, Oregon.

Some of the anecdotal illustrations in this book are true to life and are included with the permission of the persons involved. All other illustrations are composites of real situations, and any resemblance to people living or dead is coincidental.

Unless otherwise identified, all Scripture quotations in this publication are taken from the HOLY BIBLE: NEW INTERNATIONAL VERSION® (NIV®). Copyright © 1973, 1978, 1984 by International Bible Society. Used by permission of Zondervan Publishing House. All rights reserved.

Library of Congress Cataloging-in-Publication Data

Cyzewski, Ed, 1979-
  Coffeehouse theology : reflecting on God in everyday life / Ed Cyzewski.
    p. cm.
  Includes bibliographical references.
  ISBN-13: 978-1-60006-277-3
  ISBN-10: 1-60006-277-6
  1. Theology--Methodology. 2. Postmodernism--Religious aspects--Christianity. I. Title.
  BR118.C99 2008
  230--dc22

                          2008014836

Printed in the United States of America

2 3 4 5 6 7 8 / 11 10 09

To Julie

My constant reader, best friend, and love

CONTENTS

FOREWORD

I recently lost a bet to one of Ed's seminary professors, John Franke. I don't even know now what we were betting on—I think it was a Chicago Bears and Minnesota Vikings football game, but my punishment was to read John Calvin's defense of infant baptism in *The Institutes for Christian Religion*. When it comes to punishments, Franke's assignment doesn't get much better. But, besides being unconvinced by Calvin's arguments, I was overwhelmingly unconvinced by Calvin's *style of conversation*. Truth be told, I was a bit embarrassed by how Calvin berated his opponents as he blasted away at them from his bully pulpit.

Then I did what Ed is encouraging us to do in this book: I gave Calvin a break, I set Calvin in his context, and I realized that Calvin's theology was for Calvin's time. Calvin's theology, in other words, was contextually shaped. It was what Calvin heard God saying in Calvin's time and in Calvin's ways. God used Calvin to burn a hole of holiness in Switzerland and to construct a contextually shaped theology that, while clearly revealing a sixteenth-century style, has endured the test of time. In many ways, then, Calvin provides for us a model of Ed's *Coffeehouse Theology*. The best way to read Calvin is to sit behind him as he speaks, to watch how his contemporaries responded, and to see in Calvin a model of how to do the same in our world.

Which is what good theology really is. Far too often preachers and teachers find a classical theologian they love — say Athanasius or Augustine, Luther or Calvin, Wesley or Edwards. Their enthusiasm for the theologian is matched only by the dull looks they get from their congregations or classes when the teacher does whatever he or she can to teach that theology as the best form of theology ever. Which it isn't — why? Because there is no such thing as the "best form of theology ever." (Not even Calvin's, I remind my Reformed friends.) Theology is an expression of the biblical gospel and message in a specific time and for a specific time.

This kind of contextual theology is a bit like what I learned from a really good Anglican preacher. I had never heard this preacher, but I had heard what his listeners said about his sermons. So, one day in a British pub I asked him, "Can I have copies of any of your sermons?" His answer shocked me just a little less than it taught me: "I don't keep my sermons. When I leave the pulpit and enter into my study there is a dustbin. I toss the sermon in the dustbin before I begin to pray and prepare for next week's sermon."

Which also means contextual theology is so targeted that it is missional. That is, what Ed is telling us is that our reflections on God and our attempt to speak those reflections into our context are missionally shaped. They are God speaking through his Word, through his Spirit, and through a theologian who is sitting at coffee in a particular place, at a particular time, with someone listening who needs to hear that age-old biblical message in his or her way for his or her day. Once the theologian finishes his coffee, it is time to go home and let someone else sit in that same seat and talk to someone else—and do what the previous theologian did but this time for a new day and in a new way.

Which is a way of telling us that theology is a conversation—of God with the biblical authors, of the biblical authors with one another, with the early fathers with the biblical authors, and so on and on up to our own day. Most importantly, since theology is a conversation, when we pull up to the table we must invite many others, even those with whom we differ and those from global Christianity, so that together we can discern God's voice for our age. And God's Spirit hovers over all of this and does what God's Spirit always does: pierces with that Word into our heart of hearts. But only God gets the Final Word, which is his Son, and that Word has been uttered once and will be uttered even more completely at the Final Day. Until then we utter words about the Word, but our words are only words—they must not be mistaken for the Final Word.

Which leads me to a final point that I like about Ed's fine book—*Coffeehouse Theology* seeks to introduce us to where we are in history. Ed knows Calvin was a man of his time, and he knows he, too, is a man of our time. Call our time postmodernity, or if you prefer, call it late modernity. It doesn't matter what you call it. What matters is comprehending it, and Ed can help you do that. Once you know where you are in history, you are invited to pull up to the coffee table, pull out your Bible, pray for God's Spirit, know your world, and discern what God would have you say to our world.

Scot McKnight, PhD
Karl A. Olsson Professor in Religious Studies
North Park University, Chicago, Illinois

ACKNOWLEDGMENTS

This book would still be the pipe dream of a theology student were it not for the timely direction provided by my professor Dr. John Franke during hours of conversation in his office. This book began as an independent study under his direction, and I am deeply grateful for Dr. Franke's commitment to Christ, culturally informed theology, and humble scholarship. The encouragement of Spencer Burke and Bill Senyard was also indispensable.

My grandmother Phyllis Quinn has been one of my biggest supporters throughout this project, and her constant prayers have been an enormous blessing. Words cannot express how grateful I am for the manifold ways she has provided encouragement and a steady stream of requests toward heaven.

The support of my family has been tremendous. I'm grateful to my in-laws who read through early drafts—the versions I now keep under lock and key lest anyone ever read them again—and offered their comments and support. My thanks to my mother, who taught me diligence, and my father, who taught me about faith. The folks at Sanford Communications Inc. have gone above and beyond in guiding me through this entire process—from A to Z as they say—and managed to improve this book every time they touched it. My thanks go especially to David Sanford, Rebekah Clark (the fastest draw with an e-mail west of the Mississippi), Beyth Hogue, and Elizabeth Jones. It has been a joy working with NavPress, especially my acquiring editor Caleb Seeling. And I appreciate the contributions of my developmental editor, Brad Lewis, who had the uncanny ability to improve everything he touched—for that I am most grateful.

I am also grateful for all of my friends and conversation partners who helped make this book better by reading early drafts or working on some of its ideas. Though I will surely forget some of you, I would like to thank, in no particular order, Heather Cole, Nate Hulfish, Mark Willey, Josh Davidson, Eugene Miller, Heather Plier, John and Alta Ludlam, Molly Ludlam, Jack Ludlam, Roland Ludlam, Joel Ludlam, Scott Berkheimer, Makeesha Fisher, Jamie Arpin-Ricci, Spencer Burke, Adam Malliet, Derek Cooper, Bill Senyard, Adam Bennett, Jonathan Duncan, Christopher Fennig, Todd Hiestand, Adam Klein, Caitlin Bass, Lawrence Tom, and the many others who have been part of conversations both in person and online. I am also thankful for the spiritual guidance of Don and Nancy Loose, Joanne Hollway, and Hank and Jeannette Voss, and the theological guidance of my professors, Edward Meadors, William Heth, Larry Helyer, R. Todd Mangum, and David Dunbar.

I would also like to thank the kind owners of The Spiral Press (Manchester, VT), The Lawyer and the Baker (Manchester, VT), and the South Street Café (Bennington, VT) for making their establishments a safe pad for writers who need to get out of the house lest they end up puttering on household projects all day.

And of course there's my wife, Julie. Julie, without your support at crucial moments, this project would surely have failed. I can't imagine writing a book, let alone making it through the twists and turns of life, without you. You are my best critic, source of inspiration, and love of my life. It's a dream to spend my days with you reading, writing, hiking, and hanging with our rabbits—even if the rabbits are lazy freeloaders.

CONTEXTUAL THEOLOGY

Understanding Ourselves, Understanding God

When was the last time you mentioned God in a conversation, said a prayer, or read the Bible? Perhaps you were helping a friend through a rough time, asking God to protect a loved one, or studying about Jesus' ministry on earth.

God has a way of showing up in everyday life, and just about everyone believes something about God. For example, just try suggesting in a crowd of people that you think there's only one way to get to heaven. You'll hear a wide variety of opinions, often expressed with a high degree of passion. In fact, we say all kinds of things about God, such as referring to the Bible as God's Word or expressing godly views on moral issues such as poverty, war, and the protection of the unborn.

Some people believe that God acts frequently in this world, bringing peace and justice. Others see God as very angry, on the verge of raining down judgment. Still others think he set the world in motion and then walked away.

I want to know one thing: Where do these beliefs about God come from?

As a Christian, my beliefs come from the Bible—and I do believe it is inspired by God—as well as from traditions handed down from other Christians. Many Christians would agree with my list.

Even if we agree that the Bible and our traditions guide our beliefs about God, we still don't have a clear consensus about many of the particulars found in the Bible and within these traditions. Disagreements cover a range of issues such as the place of sacraments, the extent of God's control over the world, and how exactly salvation through Jesus happens. Even when we share the same sources regarding our beliefs, we have enough disagreements to drive us into thousands of different denominations.

What causes these deep divides when we try to understand God?

Maybe hidden influences change the way we read the Bible and talk about God. In fact, could our culture have a lot to do with our beliefs? People in the United States, just to name one example, have much to learn from Latin American theologians (and vice versa).

For example, think about how Christians from the U.S. and Latin America tend to read the Beatitudes (see Matthew 5:3-12; Luke 6:20-23). Most of us in the U.S spend a lot of time reading Matthew's gospel, especially 5:3 where Jesus said, "Blessed are the poor in spirit, for theirs is the kingdom of heaven." When we read these words, we think Jesus' primary concern is humility, and so we think of the poverty mentioned here as a spiritual matter. This fits well with our experience of relative wealth, power, and prosperity. Because our culture focuses on image and pride, we read Matthew and think that Jesus wants to counter our culture, teaching humility and poverty in spirit.

Something very different happens when Latin Americans read Luke's account of the Beatitudes. In Luke 6:20 Jesus said, "Blessed are you who are poor, for yours is the kingdom of God." Here Jesus speaks directly to the people, instead of *about* them as Matthew recorded. He also drops the words *in spirit*. Latin American Christians, who live amid poverty, injustice, and political turmoil, connect with the words as Luke recorded them. Here he seems to say that blessing comes from being physically poor, which is very different from the spiritual poverty in Matthew. The wealthy see blessings for the humble, while the poor see blessings for the destitute.

In these two different readings, we gain a glimpse of what happens when we read the Bible: Our local settings and cultural values—in other words, our context—influence how we read God's Word. When we read the Bible, we can't help but see God through a unique local lens.

The Bible presents a deep and rich message about God's concern for both our spiritual and physical worlds. Both interpretations are rooted in Jesus' teachings, and both are correct. However, when Christians in the United States focus solely on the spiritual message or when Latin Americans focus only on the physical part, Jesus' message loses some of its depth and richness.

UNDERSTANDING SEEKERS OF GOD

The lesson here is pretty simple: Beliefs about God change depending on context. So as we seek information about this God we want to know and to make known, we need to understand the often unde-tected influences of cultural context. The inescapable conclusion is that we're products of our times and locations, and these influences create a lens for our study of God.

All is not lost. In fact, culture is a good thing to understand.

Christians in the U.S. do need to hear Jesus' teaching about humility, and Latin American Christians do need to hear the hope of Jesus' message about the blessings promised to the physically poor. In this case, we can easily see how context becomes a valuable tool. And as we understand the values and challenges of our contexts, we can study the Bible with a greater willingness to hold our culture up to the scrutiny of God.

Of course, the danger occurs when we mistake our biblical interpretations from an isolated context as the definitive word. So we need to challenge ourselves to learn about God with an awareness of context—what we can call contextual theology—while at the same time making sure we value different insights from other cultures where Christians are learning about God in their own particular situations.

In brief, that's where we're headed together in this book. *Coffeehouse Theology* will help us form and live out contextual theology by helping us understand who we are and by including perspectives outside of our own in the midst of our study of Scripture. Together, we'll explore where our beliefs about God come from: our context, the Bible, our traditions, and Christians from other cultures.

CONCERNS ABOUT THEOLOGY AND CULTURE

We'll start with a long and hard look at who we are as theologians and the way our cultural contexts influence how we understand God. I'm not taking this approach because culture is more important than God. Rather our culture—who we are and our values—becomes both our greatest strength and largest obstacle in theology. Culture can be a strength because it serves as a tool when we use our understanding of culture to study God. Think back to the Beatitudes example: Christians in the U.S. tend to spiritualize the message of

Jesus because we understand the pride so prevalent in today's culture. Yet every culture has weaknesses. God is so much more than what we can see by ourselves. So while addressing the pride of our culture in the Beatitudes, we can easily miss out on God's concern for the poor and the blessings he sets aside for them.

You might be concerned about the amount of time we'll spend exploring the interaction of culture and theology, especially in chapters 5 and 6 on the influences of postmodernism on culture and on the church. You might already be asking, "Can't we just study the Bible and leave culture out of this? In fact, don't we just mess up the Bible by considering culture as a part of theology?" The truth is, whether we acknowledge it or not, we constantly deal with the influences of culture on theology.

Whatever philosophy dominates our culture, we can't afford to simply ignore it as we form our theology. If we do, we risk allowing the dominant philosophy to covertly influence our thinking about God. This is not to say that Christians should embrace a culture or philosophy. Instead, we should see our culture as a setting that we need to understand. Then we can either seek to overcome it or put it to use.

In fact, I want to make clear that I'm mostly ambivalent toward culture in that I don't believe one culture or philosophy is right or wrong. In chapter 3, I'll outline a number of ways we can approach the mixing of culture and theology.

Of course, this is difficult and messy work that requires practice and the input of a Christian community. However, letting an undetected culture or philosophy infect our theology can be more dangerous than ignoring culture. Here's the bottom line: If we truly want to study God, we must first understand the cultural lens that we view God through.

THEOLOGY: REFLECTING ON GOD

In light of the challenges posed by context, let's ask the question again, "Where do our beliefs about God come from?" We now understand that context plays a role, but we also need to consider specific ways we learn about God. If we want to understand where our beliefs come from, we need to understand theology (which literally means the study of God) and the role theology plays in our everyday lives.

I like to think of theology as reflecting on or thinking about God. *Reflecting* is a helpful word because it not only addresses the act of seeking an understanding of God, but it also implies the act of reflecting who God is as a result of seeking him out. In other words, theology—the act of reflecting on God—should change both how we think and how we live. We seek not to merely know *about* God but to know God in a personal and life-changing way.

Further, if we take the mission of Jesus seriously, we also reflect him for the benefit of others. Jesus instructed his followers to join his mission, to spread the good news that God isn't just present in our world but that everyone has an opportunity to know him. In this way, reflecting on God is not only essential in our own relationships with God but in our ministry to others around us and around the world. Understanding theology's place in our calling to know God and to make God known is a good place to start.

THEOLOGY IN EVERYDAY LIFE

Christians face tough questions about God all the time. One morning I walked in to work and made my usual stop in the kitchen to start brewing coffee. With that essential piece in place, I walked upstairs to my office. On the way down the hall, two of my coworkers were discussing a recent interview on a popular talk show. Joyce

Meyer, a widely known Christian writer and conference speaker, had said on this show that she believes God has forgiven her father for abusing her during childhood. If Jesus forgave this child abuser, then the way is clear for him to go to heaven. And that was the sticking point for my coworkers.

After sharing the main points of the interview, Stephanie asked me, "How could God forgive a child abuser but send a morally good atheist to hell?"

Grace is a curious thing. We love receiving it, but we really don't like seeing it given out so lavishly to others.

"I don't know if her father was sincere, but if he really did repent of his sins, change his ways, and ask God for forgiveness, then it is a very real possibility that God will save him," I replied.

"But will God send good people to hell?" she persisted.

"It's hard to say," I said. "There's a wide variety of perspectives on heaven, hell, and who goes where. Jesus did say that he is the Way, but I can't speak for what's truly in another person's heart and whether or not that person has chosen to receive God's grace. God clearly offers forgiveness to all who repent, but we can't always figure out who chooses to be with God and who rejects God."

"I just can't believe that God would forgive such a creep."

What a tough spot. I did my best to explain grace and the Cross: "I agree that it's hard to believe. But we're all separated from God by our sinful choices, and that's where Jesus comes in to conquer sin and make new life possible."

The conversation continued along similar lines. By the end of the discussion I believe that Stephanie had a clearer picture of God's grace and forgiveness, even though she kept it at a theoretical arm's length.

I'm not bringing up this incident to show how to "win" a theological discussion, but rather to show how important theology is.

When I least expected it, I walked into a very important discussion about God and salvation. That's often how theology pops up in everyday life. One moment I was carefully measuring coffee, and the next I was explaining the finer points of grace and salvation to a skeptic.

Prior to this discussion, I spent time reading the Bible, studying theology books, and interacting with Christians and non-Christians. I've weighed and wrestled with issues such as sin, grace, and forgiveness many times before Stephanie mentioned the interview that morning. Exploring our beliefs and how we form them isn't just important for a personal relationship with God but also for the way we explain God to others.

SOURCES OF THEOLOGY

After we understand the influences we face in contextual theology and the place of theology in everyday life, we're ready to look at the sources providing our beliefs about God. While most Christians begin with the Bible, we need to remember what the Bible says about itself: namely that the Holy Spirit of God provides direction and insight as we study Scripture. While anyone can read or study the Bible, Scripture itself says we need a relationship with God and a dependence on the leading of the Holy Spirit to lead us into God's truth (see John 14:26).

So, under the guidance of the Holy Spirit and with an awareness of our cultural lens, we seek to understand God by studying the Bible, our primary source for understanding God. If we ask where our beliefs come from, the Bible usually lands at the top of the list because Christians believe God inspired its writers.

After studying the Bible, we'll arrive at some conclusions. But how reliable are they? We've already looked at how people from different cultures can read the same Bible and arrive at very different conclusions. So how do we overcome the shortcomings of our context?

Thankfully, we have two allies that can help us see God in more complete ways.

First, we have the traditions of the church. These traditions uncover the ways Christians understood God in various cultures and circumstances. If we find that certain beliefs stand the test of time and hold their place in Christian theology, we can be sure they're important. For example, the Trinity, the doctrine stating that God is three persons in one substance, has withstood the scrutiny of Christians throughout history and has become a pillar of the Christian faith.

Christian tradition helps us determine what beliefs are most important, with those standing the test of time landing at the center of the faith. We can compare our beliefs today to Christian traditions and find points in history when someone took a different perspective or applied our doctrines of today in different ways. If we hold beliefs strictly unique to the present day, we should at least question why we differ from Christians before us. Perhaps we can give good reasons. However, if we're wise, we'll look to Christian tradition as a guide for what we believe today.

Second, interacting with global Christians provides another way to broaden our perspective about God and to fill in the weaknesses of our local context. As Christianity grows in Asia, Africa, Latin America, and other parts of the world, Christians in these places are all forming theology. Just as Latin American Christians broaden our understanding of Jesus' teachings about God's concern for the poor, the potential for additional insights only increases when we enter into dialogue with Christians in other contexts.

A Web of Theology

This web illustrates the interconnected nature of Christian theology's sources and contexts.

Current chapter topic will be in bold.

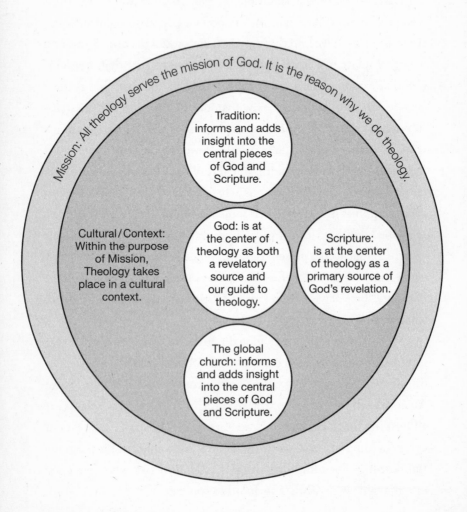

Mission: All theology serves the mission of God. It is the reason why we do theology.

Tradition: informs and adds insight into the central pieces of God and Scripture.

Cultural/Context: Within the purpose of Mission, Theology takes place in a cultural context.

God: is at the center of theology as both a revelatory source and our guide to theology.

Scripture: is at the center of theology as a primary source of God's revelation.

The global church: informs and adds insight into the central pieces of God and Scripture.

A PICTURE TO HELP US

Since we're talking about different influences on our theology, I've arranged a contextual theology web diagram that illustrates how the various parts fit together. The web appears at the end of most chapters to show how that particular topic fits into contextual theology. Because we study God within the context of our culture and God's mission to make himself known, culture and mission form circles around our web of theology, and we must take these ever-present factors in theology into account.

▶ ▶ ▶ FOR FURTHER READING

At the end of each chapter, I provide a list of suggested books for further reading. You'll probably notice that these recommendations reflect my evangelical background and draw from many authors in the missional and emerging church conversations. Of course, you can also find many excellent books beyond my list. But I've chosen to limit these recommendations to books I've read, browsed thoroughly, or at least know to be of high quality through the recommendations of trusted Christians. Keep in mind that I'm particularly concerned with contextual theology, so I haven't included many standard titles in theology studies because they don't speak to our particular focus here.

For additional resources and discussion, you can also check out my theology blog at http://inamirrordimly.com/coffeehouse-theology/introduction.

STEPPING INTO CONTEXTUAL THEOLOGY

As Christians, we can't undertake any greater quest than seeking an understanding of God. Imagine the outrage that would erupt if someone stated in a conservative church that the Bible is full of errors, or if someone suggested to a Catholic that Mary was not a virgin. Either would be as startling as replacing an opera singer at the last minute with Madonna! Our passion for our beliefs suggests that theology is a sacred and integral part of our lives, worthy of study and careful reflection.

Our understanding of God influences where we live, how we distribute our wealth, how we spend our time, who we marry, and innumerable other areas. Theology's far-reaching influence into our everyday lives calls us to a careful consideration of just where our beliefs come from. If you want to know God in deeper and richer ways than ever before, I encourage you to dig deeper into the world of contextual theology with me. As we look into who we are, who God is, and what historic and global Christians have to teach us, our conversations, prayers, Bible studies, and relationships with others will be far richer than we could ever imagine.

Chapter 1

MISSION

Why the Church Needs Theology

I remember my own moment of salvation. When I prayed to receive Christ, I answered the essential Mac truck of a question asked by most Christians I knew: "If you were to die tonight, do you know for sure that you would go to heaven?"

Questions like that have a way of stopping a conversation. (Now that I think about it, I don't know why the dying always had to happen at night. Perhaps night is just more frightening, especially after watching subtly terrifying movies like *Signs*. I can't tell you how relieved I am that we no longer have a shed in our yard where I can see an imaginary alien stalking along the roof.)

My moment of salvation also involved a simple drawing of a vast sin chasm that separated me from God. You might remember a similar presentation, with the bridges of works and religious efforts falling short of spanning the gap between you on one bank and heaven on the other side. My salvation appeared hopeless until John 3:16

permitted the drawing of a large cross to fill the entire gap of sin separating me from God.

With my own eternal destination secure, heaven pushed its way to the forefront of my spirituality. Nothing was more important than securing the safe, heavenly passage of souls. I remember trying to share the gospel in spite of my quaking nerves and sweaty palms. I remember steering a conversation with my auto mechanic about replacing my timing belt to eternal issues. Even now, somewhere in Pennsylvania, a mechanic probably remembers an awkward conversation with a nervous seminary student every time he works on a timing belt.

These approaches to presenting the gospel remind me of a statement I once heard from a self-proclaimed agnostic: "Christianity and every other religion aims to control people by determining where they go after they die. Christians are obsessed with going to heaven."

This provocative statement squarely hits on the importance of theology both as we walk with the Lord and in our call to share the gospel. Is the gospel simply a message about how to get to heaven? Or does it also hold a message for the here and now that radically changes how we should live?

What can help us understand the salvation God offers through the death and resurrection of Jesus? I believe the answer is theology. Christ's saving acts established his lordship not just in heaven but also on earth, and his actions form the content of the gospel we preach and practice. Before returning to heaven, Jesus left his followers with a mission to take his message to the ends of the earth. Without theology as a guide, we run the risk of missing out on the good news of God not only for ourselves but for all people who need to hear this message about God's love for us.

Theology plays a significant role not only in helping us understand the gospel in a life-changing way but also in how we carry this message of salvation to others and take our place in God's mission.

WHERE DOES THEOLOGY FIT IN?

Theology determines the content of the gospel we believe, the way in which we share the gospel, and who we share this good news with. Our ability to faithfully form theology and then to put it into practice can either help or hinder our ability to carry out our mission to share the good news of Christ.

Each of us reflects on God — or each of us does theology — simply to carry on the mission of Jesus that began with his incarnation, continued through his ministry, and that he passed on to us before he ascended. The core of this mission brings humanity into relationship with God and under his caring rule. So we dig into theology both for the sake of our own walk with the Lord and for the sake of the world that needs to hear his message.

Theology becomes our tool to help explain the gospel to anyone with a question or challenge (see 1 Peter 3:14-16). We can't simply answer these questions with "Jesus once gave me the warm fuzzies when I prayed." Instead, we need solid theological content to connect with our experiences of God. We can't risk placing ourselves or anyone else at the mercy of a gospel message we don't think through completely or simply pass on as a matter of doctrinal hearsay.

TAKING RESPONSIBILITY FOR THE GOSPEL

I can't remember the exact moment this thought hit me, but it was sometime during my college years. While reading through one of Paul's epistles, I realized that I didn't understand why Jesus went through all the trouble of raising himself from the dead — however that worked. Somehow, I'd heard a lot about the cross, the blood, and the nails. But in spite of all the preaching, teaching, and singing I'd experienced in several different churches, I'd never really heard much about the third day. Lyrics such as "Calvary covered it all," "the Cross has done it all," "the nails in his hands," and so on, filled the worship slides on Sunday mornings. But the significance of Easter morning hopped by somewhere between the stations of the cross and a chocolate rabbit.

Of course, the Resurrection is a fairly important doctrine. Paul said that if Christ weren't really raised from the dead, then we are to be pitied (see 1 Corinthians 15:17-19). So I felt a little disturbed about my realization. With Bible in hand, I began diving in to all of the relevant passages regarding the Resurrection. I looked into a few of the creeds that affirm Christ's resurrection. Over coffee or dinner and during work, I kept my Christian friends and my family up to date on the progress of my study.

After typing out my half-processed thoughts on my computer, I set to work posting the findings online at my blog, http:// inamirrordimly.com. This took the study up a notch, as my friends and fellow bloggers heard plenty about my search for answers and added their own thoughts to my study. After a few weeks of agonizing over this important event and doctrine, I came to the conclusion that the Resurrection is the perfect flipside of the Cross. Let me explain.

Jesus' crucifixion on the cross is clearly a highly significant event. In the mold of the Passover lamb found in the book of Exodus (see Exodus 12; 2 Chronicles 35:1-19) or a sacrificial offering prescribed in Leviticus, Jesus died on the cross as the perfect sin offering for all humanity. In fact, Jesus' agonized cry, "It is finished," is his declaration of triumph over the powers of death. It marks the dawn of a wonderful new era when Jesus himself mediates our relationship with God and his resurrection becomes the beginning of that new life and new creation with God. The Cross was the end; the Resurrection is the new beginning.

At the end of my study, I discovered a new challenge to submit to the rule of Christ and to receive the new life he made possible with his resurrection. For example, my prayer life changed radically in the light of the Resurrection. Instead of only asking for God's forgiveness and protection from sin, I began to claim God's victory over sin so I could live in that reality after repenting. The new life provided by Christ became my protection from sin. To paraphrase Paul, I'd died to sin and risen with Christ (see Romans 6:2,7,10), and now I lived under his protective rule.

I realized that it's just the first step to kneel before the cross and claim Christ's power over sin. God gives us so much more; he wants us to emerge from the nails and blood and begin a new life under his rule. In fact, I believe neglecting the Resurrection is one of the key reasons many Christians don't live in the freedom and power of God. In other words, many Christians still live in slavery to sin, still obeying the desires of an old nature that died with Jesus on the cross. But with his death and resurrection, we actually become new people. Perhaps no truth is more important than the Resurrection when we want to talk about living a new life in the freedom of Christ.

Besides the personal ramifications, my rediscovery of the Resurrection radically changed how I shared the gospel. The gospel no longer represented a simple cure for sin at the foot of the cross. It became a much larger story with the Cross at center stage, but not stealing the show. I could share the desire of God to be reunited with his creation and his plan to bring such a reunion about in the Cross *and* Resurrection. Instead of hammering a bleak message that ended on Good Friday, I could end with the hope of new life and restoration.

THE MISSION OF THE CHURCH

I'm telling you about my search for the significance of Christ's resurrection because I think it demonstrates our responsibility to understand our doctrines and beliefs. As Christians, our theology is a key part of who we are. Understanding what we believe fits squarely into the mission of the church to know God and to make him known. Everything we hold true about God and our Christian faith has been taken from the Bible by someone and taken root as a doctrine.

We form theology to guide us into a closer relationship with the true God and to provide motivation and direction for sharing the gospel. Both of these purposes tie directly into the mission of Jesus, a mission that revolved around revealing God. Jesus' stories about sowing seeds and letting our light shine are all gentle hints about his mission to teach us about God and to restore a relationship between the Creator and all humanity. When Jesus told his followers, "As the Father has sent me, I am sending you" (John 20:21), that same mission became the main reason for leaving his church in the world. God is already at work in our world. We need to decide if we want to join his mission.

While we might think of mission set apart as missionaries taking the gospel to foreign people or providing physical and spiritual relief to people in an impoverished area, the truth is that Jesus sends out the entire church to make disciples, and to bring good news — physical and spiritual — to the poor. The mission of being "sent out" changes the church from an outside-in to an inside-out approach. Instead of asking how we can get people into church, mission asks how we can get church to the people. God is working all over creation, drawing people in, waiting for us to go out and join in this work. As Christians, we're not called to sit and wait, but to go and tell. However, if we don't take the time to know God through the task of theology, then we won't be formed into God's kind of people, and we won't be able to bring redemptive action and a redemptive message when we go.

In other words, we should always link theology to the work of living out the gospel and drawing people to God. While we form theology for our own spiritual growth, we should also form theology to be transformed into God's people who demonstrate God to others and to respond to questions about God that arise every day among those who don't yet know him.

When we view theology in this light, we also happen to obey Jesus' essential commands to love God and to love one another. We reflect on God because we love him and want to know him better. At the same time, we reveal God to others by living in God's truth because we want the very best for them—the freedom and life that come from knowing God.

ORGANIZING OUR THEOLOGY

Now that we understand how theology lies at the very core of what it means to be Christians who are committed to joining the mission of God, let's briefly break down the different kinds of theology we might run into. Most experts place a word in front of the word *theology* to more accurately describe these different ways to organize Christian doctrine.

Each branch of theology plays a role in how we understand God and share the gospel. Just so we're on the same page, I'll briefly explain biblical theology, systematic theology, and contextual theology. However, as you read on, you'll quickly see that forming and doing contextual theology serves as the main thrust of the rest of our discussion.

Biblical Theology

Biblical theology organizes beliefs about God around the writers of Scripture. For example, if you've heard a series of sermons on the writings of the apostle Paul or the apostle John, you've been a part of one example of biblical theology. Or if you study all the books of a biblical writer such as Luke, who wrote the gospel bearing his name and the Acts of the Apostles, you're using biblical theology to organize your study of God.

At a more detailed level, biblical theology seeks to understand the stories and letters found in the Bible in their historical settings. In addition, biblical theologians study the books of the Bible according to their literary type. For example, a pastor might begin a sermon on the Epistles of Paul by comparing them with other epistles from that time in history. The final conclusions reached in biblical theology are typically arranged according to the points made within the context of each biblical book.

Systematic Theology

Systematic theology organizes beliefs about God according to our contemporary categories. For example, if you've ever heard a sermon series on contemporary topics such as what the Bible says about cheating, lying, love, or grace, you've taken part in forming systematic theology.

While systematic theology doesn't ignore the unique elements of each biblical writer and book, it does require pulling verses from a variety of different books and arranging them under topical headings.

Contextual Theology

Just like biblical and systematic theology, contextual theology relies on the Bible as the primary source for information about God. However, contextual theology also recognizes that all theology takes place within a local cultural context. This cultural context colors our reading of the Bible and produces a wide variety of locally made theologies. Contextual theology also reminds us that each local understanding of God has strengths and weaknesses, and we can fill in some of these holes by listening to other local theologies. In the introduction, for example, we looked at how the contextual theologies of Latin America and North America can inform each other about God's blessings for the humble and God's blessings for the poor.

PUTTING THEOLOGY TO WORK

If theology helps us understand the content of the gospel message as we join the mission of God, then using contextual theology will help us be certain that our beliefs don't contain any massive blind spots. Contextual theology makes us aware of the particular challenges we face in our unique situations and ensures that our understanding of God not only speaks to the needs of that context, but also takes into account the enriching insights of Christians from other contexts.

Whether we're trying to figure out the complete message of the gospel or addressing the concerns of a skeptic fed up with the obsession of Christians with heaven, theology serves as an indispensable tool. As we put theology to work, we'll require some simple steps to guide us through the influences of cultural context and other sources that fill in the details about God. Let's look at that next.

▶ ▶ ▶ FOR FURTHER READING

- *Missional Church: A Vision for the Sending of the Church in North America* (Grand Rapids: Eerdmans, 1998), edited by Darrell Guder
- *Exiles: Living Missionally in a Post-Christian Culture* (Peabody, MA: Hendrickson, 2006), by Michael Frost
- *Transforming Mission: Paradigm Shifts in Theology of Mission* (Maryknoll, NY: Orbis Books, 1991), by David J. Bosch

- *Believing in the Future: Toward a Missiology of Western Culture* (Leominster, England: Gracewing, 2005), by David J. Bosch
- *The Shaping of Things to Come: Innovation and Mission for the Twenty-first Century Church* (Peabody, MA: Hendrickson, 2003), by Alan Hirsch and Michael Frost

For additional resources and discussion, see http://inamirrordimly .com/coffeehouse-theology/chapter-1.

A Web of Theology

This web illustrates the interconnected nature of Christian theology's sources and contexts.

Current chapter topic will be in bold.

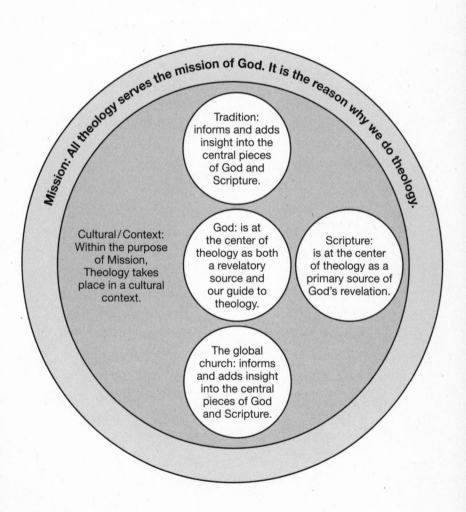

Mission: All theology serves the mission of God. It is the reason why we do theology.

Tradition: informs and adds insight into the central pieces of God and Scripture.

Cultural / Context: Within the purpose of Mission, Theology takes place in a cultural context.

God: is at the center of theology as both a revelatory source and our guide to theology.

Scripture: is at the center of theology as a primary source of God's revelation.

The global church: informs and adds insight into the central pieces of God and Scripture.

Chapter 2

BEYOND OURSELVES TO A COFFEEHOUSE THEOLOGY

While growing up Catholic and then casting my lot with the Baptists, I used to think God voted Republican. I consistently sided with the pro-life, anti-evolution, tax-cutting moral majority throughout high school and college. During my senior year at a Christian high school, students presented papers on topics near to their hearts. The selection of topics ran like the speaking points at the Republican convention: anti-evolution, pro-death penalty, anti–affirmative action, and anti-welfare programs that funded the loafers who wouldn't pitch in and do their share. Our middle-class God looked on approvingly from a Republican red sunset, showering us with the blessings of material prosperity. Never mind what a Christian Democrat would say—let alone a liberation theologian from Latin America. We just knew we were on God's side.

My friends and I couldn't conceive of a God who'd approve of the so-called "poor stewardship" of government programs aimed at helping the poor or who'd want to spare hardened criminals a well-deserved jolt on the electric chair. What's more, how could God approve of the violent snuffing out of an unborn life or the teaching of scientific theories that shoved him out of the picture? Of course God had our back!

We were like what essayist and outspoken fan of Jesus Anne Lamott quotes her friend Tom as saying, "You can safely assume you've created God in your own image when it turns out he hates all of the same people you do."[1]

Ten years after presenting our senior papers, I caught up with some of my high school friends. We could only think of one person from our class who still held to the same perspective presented in his senior paper,[2] the guy who asserted that large box stores such as Home Depot and Wal-Mart destroy American communities. I can't speak for all of my friends, but I know that during the ten years that had passed since high school, I had come to grips with some of the complexities of our cultural setting and realized that God's side is very hard to define.

Looking back, I can see a lot more clearly that factors from our context exerted a huge influence on our views about God and Scripture. The views we labeled as God's more likely grew out of our middle-class, conservative culture. Now I realize that while we might agree or disagree about the views, we should all agree that we have a problem when we make God the approving leader of these views—because this kind of mistake can dramatically skew the way we read the Bible and apply it.

We can go about theology in a variety of ways, but we need to include some basic components to make sure we come to accurate conclusions. We don't want to overlook gaping blind spots or make the same mistakes Christians made in the past. Whether we form theology out of a study of the Bible (biblical theology) or start our theology by studying a particular issue or concern (systematic theology), we also need to take into account our own culture as well as the revelation of God, the Bible, Christian history, and the global church. This means that serious study of God consists of two steps: knowing ourselves and knowing God.

GETTING BEYOND OURSELVES

In my childhood home, Jesus looked down on our living room from his perch at the top of the steps. Waves of brown hair floated over his shoulders and his sharp brown eyes met mine every time I went to my bedroom. And even if the brown hair in the portrait comes fairly close to reality, I later realized that the soft white skin of the Jesus in the painting wasn't quite right for a man born in the Middle East. Of course, other paintings even depict Jesus with blond hair and blue eyes—maybe proving the point that we enjoy creating God in our own image.

Just as we often picture Jesus looking just like us, we also like the Bible to look just like the way we live our lives. We tend to interpret what Scripture says to our own liking. At times, of course, the Bible speaks clearly on particular topics. Yet any time we jump into the Bible and begin laying out doctrine to the tune of "This is exactly what the Bible says," we enter potentially dangerous territory. So when we approach theology, we need to take the crucial first step of making sure we understand ourselves and our context. Only when we appropriately measure our strengths and potential biases— misunderstandings that we bring to the process of forming theology —can we proceed to the second step of reflecting on God.

By the way, I'm not accusing anyone of deliberately setting out to be narrow minded. It simply happens to all of us at one time or another because we can't help loving how we see the world.

Perspective is a funny thing. The radio show *Marketplace* interviewed a number of wealthy parents and their children, asking them how they handled the demands of parenthood and childhood with all of those extra bucks lying around. One woman on the program took issue with the label "wealthy." The host of the show went in for the kill by politely asking, "How many homes do you own?"

After a long pause—as if she needed her fingers, toes, or gold bricks to count—the woman whispered, "Let's see, one, two, three, four . . . five. Yes, five. That's five that we actively own." I'm not sure where her cutoff for "wealthy" falls. Perhaps at lucky seven. But this woman had clearly lost touch with the average American's struggle to own one home, let alone the working poor's difficulties in finding a feasible rental property. Even my 1,000 square-foot home—one of the cheapest places in our community—makes my family wealthy when compared to a large segment of the world's population. When it comes to perspective, we need to get beyond our own narrow view of both God and the world. This not only keeps us from looking foolish when we reflect on God, it also allows us to know and experience him in a richer and more accurate light.

THE RAW ELEMENTS OF THEOLOGY

Once we start to understand that God isn't exactly like us—that he's not made in our image—then we've made good progress. If we know a little about who we are and some of the ways we can misrepresent God, we're well on our way. You might call this new awareness humility.

In light of this newfound humility, we can more accurately reflect on who God is, and we can more honestly look at our own culture and other sources and how they affect our reflection of God. Let's briefly look at both of these elements of theology.

Reflecting on God

As we move on to the true work of theology, knowing God, we're wise if we examine the ways we reflect on him. As Christians, most of us learn how to study God in our churches. Small groups, Sunday school classes, informal discussions over coffee, and special classes for people interested in following Christ but who haven't yet made a commitment to him typically provide the first clues on how we study God.

The first time I truly studied the Bible and gathered clues about God was at the age of sixteen. God had some pretty tough competition at that point in my life, and my wise pastor gathered together a group of us hormone-pumping, girl-watching men-in-waiting for a study of 3 John. While some groups plow through this tiny book in one study, we took several meetings to unravel the context and contents of this letter.

I'm a little embarrassed to write this now, but I remember being surprised that the Bible actually talked about events that were . . . real. I had always pictured Jesus preaching on a hill to eerily silent masses or a prophet like Elijah smiting someone in otherworldly, almost mythical, scenarios. While I believed the Bible was true, I didn't expect it to resemble real life. But that's exactly what I learned as our pastor led us through this study.

The apostle John wrote his third letter to Gaius, who had some health issues and who had to deal with Diotrophes—a guy who abused his leadership power in Gaius's church. Based on what we know from other books of the Bible, many Christian preachers in the first century traveled from town to town around the Mediterranean Sea to share the good news. While many had pure motives, others were in it for the money—something I still find shocking when the church was so young and without significant resources. Still, churches needed to show hospitality to these ministers, as all shared a part in God's work.

However, Diotrophes had his own plans. John pointed out the trouble that Diotrophes was causing:

> I wrote to the church, but Diotrephes, who loves to be first, will have nothing to do with us. So if I come, I will call attention to what he is doing, gossiping maliciously about us. Not satisfied with that, he refuses to welcome the brothers. He also stops those who want to do so and puts them out of the church. (3 John 9-10)

We couldn't believe that people in the early church struggled with cliques, popularity contests, and talking behind each other's backs. It sounded just like our high school! The Bible—or at least this little piece of it—jumped light years ahead in relevance, because we could relate to it and apply what it said to our lives. I began to realize that God has something to say to us and we should take his book seriously.

Of course, learning about God is a clumsy, long-term process. That little group study was only the first step of many, but it succeeded in pushing us to the most important part of theology: studying the Bible. As we immersed ourselves in God's story, his Spirit used the raw materials in the pages of Scripture to teach and transform us.

At this point, I do need to note one important caution: While the Bible rests firmly at the center of Christian theology, we need to remember that the Bible is about God. And if God provides his Word to reveal himself to us, it stands to reason that God himself plays a vital role in our study of Scripture. He does this by guiding us to truth through the Holy Spirit.

In other words, our study of God begins with a relationship with God. I believe that Christian theology can't proceed without the leading of the Holy Spirit. While anyone can reflect on God, a theology that claims to be *Christian* must have a connection with this divine direction. God's revealed love for me drives me on in theology, making it an awesome experience rather than a begrudged chore. Without his love moving me, guiding me, and empowering me, I might as well instead fill my time with mountains to climb, books to read, and a thousand other topics to blog about.

The Ongoing Work of Theology

While our chief source for reflecting on God is obviously the Bible (under the guidance and leading of the Holy Spirit), we can bring balance to our Bible study by also consulting other sources. We should never think of these additional sources, such as the historic church and the global church, as equal to Scripture. But they offer invaluable advice and direction, and in particular, our traditions shape how we read the Bible today, so we're wise to learn about them. Think of it this way: While a few Christian thinkers might have an original thought, chances are good that someone in church history or in another country has already wrestled with it and might have a helpful or insightful perspective to offer.

If you're overwhelmed with the enormity of contextual theology, I have good news. Theology isn't a one-shot deal, a test that we either pass or fail. Rather, theology is something we take with us into our everyday lives and constantly reconsider and revise—an ongoing process that evolves through an interactive relationship with God, the Bible, the traditions of the church, and the global church.

As we seek to know God and to share his gospel, we enter into a constant dialogue with these sources, always refining, developing, and reviewing. We don't finish theology like a work of art that we then stand back to admire. Quite frankly, God is far too complex and our world far too uncertain for that. If I can stretch the metaphor a little, I prefer to think of theology as a collaborative and ongoing street mural that exists for the benefit of everyone in a locality. The earthy, communal, and local quality of this art form captures some clues concerning how we proceed with theology. Realizing that we're never quite done is the key. New issues will arise and fresh perspectives will emerge, always calling us to draw anew from God's revelation. We're never finished with sifting through Scripture to find out what God thinks and says about those issues and perspectives.

As Christians, we keep in touch with the important issues of our times by immersing ourselves in our surroundings as God's representatives. We then bring the proclamations and changes of the kingdom to our times and surroundings. David Dunbar, my professor in seminary, often spoke of congregations as outposts for God's mission in the world, sending-off points where we regroup and refuel before going out as God's ambassadors. I find that a helpful way to think about the role of Christian communities and the place where theology takes place. Both individually and through our congregations, we heed the call of following Jesus and complete the mission of embodying and sharing the news of God's coming rule in the person of Jesus. If we want to be God's agents sent out from these outposts into the world, then we need an awareness regarding the spirit of the age and the prevailing views of people in our contexts.

Then, when false doctrines emerge either within or outside the church, we can practice sound theology and address the issues in question when we regroup in our congregations. For example, perhaps the most popular heresy to take hold in the early twenty-first century is the alternative Christianity advocated by Dan Brown in *The Da Vinci Code*. I remember a pastor telling me about a casual conversation he'd had with someone who said, "This book changed my life!" Having not read Brown's landmark book, the pastor felt unable to make a strong response—something I hold to his credit since it's easy to condemn what we don't understand or know little about on a firsthand basis. What's more, he promptly went to work looking into the book's storyline and theological teachings. Of course, what he discovered was quite disturbing because, in case you don't know, Brown tells the story of Jesus' romantic love for Mary Magdalene and a convoluted cult of Magdalene worship that somehow combines every secret society and validates every crackpot conspiracy theory since the first century.

Of course, I'm exaggerating. But I'm not far off the mark! After finding that such a story gained a prominent position in today's culture and even among people he meets every day, this pastor (and many other Christians) committed himself to sound theology and reviewing his church history in the midst of a false doctrine that rose in worldly esteem.[3]

In many ways, the reason for contextual theology hasn't changed since the days of the early Christians, who typically formed theology in response to heresy, controversial doctrines, or challenging issues in particular cultures. When we view theology in this light, we can easily see that the study of God shouldn't be reserved for the halls of seminaries or for theological bookworms with mountains of books in their homes — not that there's anything wrong with having a lot of theology books.[4] The point is that when theology aims to address the issues of our time and the false doctrines clamoring for airtime in our congregations, every Christian needs to take a place at the table. When we form a "coffeehouse theology" that explores God's perspective on contemporary issues, we can more effectively share the gospel with the world and cling to our God. We need each other because we'll never have a complete perspective beyond error. In addition, we never complete the task of forming theology because our world always changes and we'll always find a new fad to address.

As Christians, we can connect with theology in a number of ways, especially since the Internet has become increasingly popular and user friendly. We can access theological libraries and numerous perspectives with the help of a computer and an Internet connection. At the same time, our interconnected world also means that false teachings and views counter to the gospel can spread quickly. In other words, truth and lies can spread equally fast. The question we must answer is, as individual Christians and collectively as the church, will we take our place in today's culture to share the good news of God's kingdom?

FROM THE COFFEEHOUSE TO REAL LIFE

One of my favorite examples of contextual theology comes from the contrast between American and Latin American theology. Experiencing the contrast between these two contextual theologies firsthand profoundly changed my life.

As many good changes do, it all started with a weakness. In my case, the weakness was my unabashed love for any book whose title begins with "The Cambridge Companion to . . ." I'd just picked up *The Cambridge Companion to Evangelical Theology* (Cambridge: Cambridge University Press, 2007), replacing *Julie and Julia* (a great read for another time) on my nightstand. The sections on African, Asian, and Latin American theology sucked me in, and in no time I found myself immersed in the insights of contextual theologians all around the world.

I could dig out some relevant quotes, but this is the gist of what they said: "God is concerned about the poor, so we're concerned about the poor." This one thought stuck in my mind: *If God is concerned about the poor, I don't understand why I'm not.*

It was disturbing enough to realize that I wasn't on the same page as God. But I found it far worse to discover that I was also ambivalent about changing how I felt. I don't even know if *ambivalent* is the right word. The idea of caring about the poor simply didn't connect to my American theology.

Spurred on by the articles in my *Cambridge Companion to Evangelical Theology*, I looked into passages in the Bible about the poor. Sure enough, I discovered verses all over Scripture about God's concern for the poor and his upholding of justice for everyone. "God cares about the poor, and so should you," practically leapt off the page, but I still didn't get it. This time of engaging in contextual or coffeehouse theology demonstrated God's concern for the poor, but I just couldn't force it into my heart to make myself care. What else could I do but act out of obedience to what I knew?

Using some connections in the nonprofit sector in my community and abroad, I began offering my services to a number of groups. Everyone I spoke with was thrilled to hear I wanted to help, but inevitably they either didn't need me at the current time or failed to follow up. Here I was, trying to obey God by offering my services, but no one seemed interested. To a certain degree, I felt relieved. "Well, God, I gave it a go, but I guess the poor aren't interested in my help."

Not quite.

Not long after my half-hearted venture into the world of volunteering among the poor, I read an article in *Christianity Today* where a theologian from Latin America stated that the poor don't want wealthy Americans to feel bad about their prosperity; they want the rich and powerful to use their influence and positions to improve the lot of the poor.[5] Perhaps guilt over my own wealth, although meager by American standards, was cutting off my head knowledge about the poor from my heart. Perhaps I just needed some direction to put my concern for the poor into action. To this day, I don't understand why that article mattered so much to me. But after reading it, a wave of understanding rushed over me. I cared for the poor.

The very next day, I received two phone calls asking for my help with nonprofit groups in my community. I said yes, and I really meant it.

As we learn about God in our contexts and include perspectives outside our own, we find the heart of coffeehouse theology, a way of reflecting on God in everyday life that takes our context seriously. Coffeehouse theology stretches what we know about God and forces us into uncomfortable territory. We just might rediscover our God, and as we reflect on him we'll also begin to reflect him without even realizing it.

▶ ▶ ▶ FOR FURTHER READING

- *Who Needs Theology? An Invitation to the Study of God* (Downers Grove, IL: InterVarsity, 1996), by Stanley Grenz and Roger Olson
- *The Character of Theology: An Introduction to Its Nature, Task, and Purpose* (Grand Rapids, MI: Baker, 2005), by John Franke
- *Theology: The Basics* (Malden, MA: Wiley-Blackwell, 2007), by Alister E. McGrath
- *Christian Theology* (Grand Rapids, MI: Baker, 1998), by Millard J. Erickson
- *Theology for the Community of God* (Grand Rapids, MI: Eerdmans, 2000), by Stanley Grenz

For additional resources and discussion, see http://inamirrordimly.com/coffeehouse-theology/chapter-2.

Chapter 3

CHRISTIANITY AND CULTURE

Hoping to bump into Bethlehem probably wasn't the smartest thing I've ever done.

But like the friends I was with during the second week of our semester abroad, I was intoxicated with the land of Israel. By the time we decided to hike south to Bethlehem, our group had grown to about thirty people. Without benefit of a map, compass, or common sense, we just walked south and hoped to find the city known as the birthplace of Jesus.

We fancied ourselves quite rugged. Unfortunately, ruggedness doesn't guarantee success, and we spent a *lot* of time walking through suburbs, wandering around hills, and avoiding shepherds who wanted nothing to do with us. And as we drew closer to a predominantly Palestinian section of the city, we ran into a problem.

Before departing, some people more familiar with the culture advised us that the women must wear dresses or at least pants, because some men view women in shorts as "loose." In fact, we were told the men shouldn't show off their legs either. Of course, one of the women in our group *was* wearing shorts and lacked a contingency plan. It was so hot that I could have branded cattle with the visor of my hat, so I wore shorts, but I carried pants in my backpack. To aid the damsel in distress, I handed over my pants, setting myself up to feel eerily odd when I pranced into Bethlehem—legs bared in all their glory. *Every* man there wore pants!

To make matters more awkward, I like to sit with one leg crossed over the other. This was another bad idea because apparently showing off the sole of my shoe to a passerby is the equivalent of giving the middle finger (at least that's what I was told at the time). So the entire time I sat in a café in Bethlehem, I had to keep reminding myself that both feet belonged flat on the floor.

Fortunately, in spite of my bare legs and paranoia about inadvertently flipping off someone with the sole of my shoe, we had a wonderful visit to Bethlehem and only positive experiences with the people there. We drank fresh orange juice in the café and spent the rest of our time exploring the beautiful stone streets just days before the intifada in the fall of 2000 that essentially closed this town off from the world for several years.

CULTURE: WHO WE ARE AND HOW WE SEE THE WORLD

This ill-conceived hiking trip illustrates how ingrained culture is for all people around the world. Culture is "the way of life, especially the general customs and beliefs, of a particular group of people at a particular time."[1] In other words, culture is who we are, what we do, and what we believe. We could speak of the colorful festivals and unique food of Mexican culture. A youth culture exists today that makes body image and musical taste top priorities. And we live amid a pop culture with famous self-help authors, daytime TV stars, and an assortment of celebrities and vices.

In *Coffeehouse Theology*, I want us to think about culture in the broadest of terms: the values, language, and customs of a nation or people group. Within each nation, culture evolves over time, customs change, and people adopt different values. For example, Americans in the 1930s learned to save and scrape during the Great Depression, but by the 1950s the culture had changed into a consumer society with a sudden boom in wealth. While subcultures exist, examining the larger features of our times will help us most as we seek to understand God in a particular time and place.

So we can agree that we're situated in a culture, and in large part, culture determines how we interpret actions such as wearing shorts or crossing one leg over the other. In American culture, these actions are neutral, but among Palestinians, the same actions are considered disrespectful or inappropriate. What's more, if each culture has a unique collection of values, beliefs, and practices, just how can Christians go about forming theology within a particular culture that will no doubt influence how we read the Bible? While a culture's views on the length of your pants won't come up when reading the Bible, the way our culture defines morality or truth or regards the spiritual realm will play a significant role in how we read the Bible.

When it comes to Christians and their thoughts about God, we can't expect one specific culture to give us a complete picture. And what really matters is communicating God's truth in a culturally relevant way while still challenging the parts of culture that can't be reconciled with God. I like to call this our prophetic calling. As Christians, if we want to understand God in a particular culture (which is a basic definition of contextual theology), we need to balance the need for relevant terms, concepts, and methods with the *prophetic* task of delivering God's values and truth.

For example, one missionary to Japan shared the difficulty of explaining the monotheistic Christian God in a culture that lacks the concept of monotheism and an equivalent word for "God." Because of the cultural differences, he explained God to a Japanese audience in a significantly different way than he would to an American audience, yet he still challenged the Japanese culture by introducing his listeners to the one true God.

Americans run into similar disconnects—although on a somewhat smaller scale—when well-meaning congregations continue to use old methods of sharing the gospel. We can see the influence of cultural context in our history by recalling the revivals and tent meetings that were extremely effective ways of teaching the gospel throughout much of America's history. But in the wake of Billy Graham's retirement—just to choose a rough end point—significant segments of the world have changed. In the midst of pluralism, skepticism about salvation through Christ alone, and even a general distrust of religious authorities, we need to rethink the top-down and one-way communication of revivals. We still need to share the truth of the gospel, but how we communicate that message of truth changes in light of our culture.

THE FIRST CONTEXTUAL THEOLOGIANS

So here we are: We're aware of the way culture affects and influences theology, but we need some practical steps to do this thing called contextual theology. I believe anyone can become a contextual theologian in two steps.

First, we can learn from the original and best contextual theologians. We can likely find the work of these theologians on the bookshelves and coffee tables of every Christian. I'm talking about the writers of the Bible, who provide excellent examples of contextual theology. They successfully explain God in a particular time and place while balancing a message that was both relevant and prophetic. As we study their writing, we can find some excellent clues on how culture mixes with our study of God.

Second, we need to follow in the footsteps of Scripture's writers and learn about our own cultures. We need to look at the strengths and weaknesses of our cultures and determine those parts we can use and the parts we have to confront. When we understand some of the elements of culture—who we are, how we think, and what we value—we prepare ourselves to not just use the tools of our culture to speak about God, we can also spot the parts of our culture opposed to God that need to be hit with the prophetic challenge of God's vision and values.

With these two steps in mind, let's start our journey into contextual theology by looking at some examples from the Bible.

Experiences of the Times

Although Scripture is relevant for today and speaks directly to us in many ways, it also was written to specific people groups in various points of history. The Bible contains a cultural context all its own. So we can't just think about the influence of our own culture when we read and interpret the Bible; we also need to consider the culture that existed during the writing of each book. The writers of Scripture formed their own kind of contextual theology that shared the story of God using the literary forms, language, and shared experiences of their times. Using these familiar tools, they spoke to the issues of their times, challenged the parts of their culture that opposed God, and—above all—communicated the gospel.

In addition, the Bible shows how God sent people into their cultures to communicate his message, just as God sends us out of our comfort zones and into the world. In one of the first conversations after his resurrection, Jesus declares, "Peace be with you! As the Father has sent me, I am sending you" (John 20:21). Again, in the book of Acts, Jesus explains, "You will receive power when the Holy Spirit comes on you; and you will be my witnesses in Jerusalem, and in all Judea and Samaria, and to the ends of the earth" (Acts 1:8).

Jesus was born and lived in the time and place of a hellenized and Roman-controlled Israel that still felt the shockwaves of the exile rumbling through its religious and political life. Jesus operated within his time, teaching in parables and attending the synagogue like other Jews. Yet his enmeshment with his times didn't detract from his message regarding the kingdom of God. Similarly, as disciples of Christ, our trajectory is outward, entangled in the culture that surrounds us.

Jesus challenged the cultural expectations surrounding lepers, prostitutes, and other untouchables of his day. He healed on the Sabbath and declared all food clean, while advocating that the Law would never be repealed. Jesus simultaneously attacked and affirmed the Jewish culture of the New Testament times. We see the very Spirit of Christ in the apostle Paul's words:

> To the Jews I became like a Jew, to win the Jews. To those under the law I became like one under the law (though I myself am not under the law), so as to win those under the law. To those not having the law I became like one not having the law (though I am not free from God's law but am under Christ's law), so as to win those not having the law. (1 Corinthians 9:20-21)

Just as the early church determined very different ways to explain the gospel to the Jews (in Acts 2) and the Greeks (in Acts 17), we should always be looking to understand and express our faith within a particular cultural context.

The Language of the Culture

The gospel of John might be one of the most familiar examples of how to form contextual theology. John's book has a unique vocabulary, order of events, and way of referring to Jesus, all quite unlike the three other gospels. Throughout the narrative, John makes numerous references to light and dark, including the presentation of Jesus as the true light. An unspecified darkness misunderstands the light. But why does John use such mysterious language? Why not simply make a straightforward statement about Jesus?

When we look back at the cultural context when John wrote his gospel, we quickly see that he was a brilliant contextual theologian — a coffeehouse theologian even before Turkish coffee caught on. A popular philosophy taught during John's time divided the world into two distinct spheres: good and evil. People saw all physical matter as evil, while everything spiritual was good. Some described this separation in terms of light (the good spiritual realm) and darkness (the evil physical realm).[2] So this light-darkness perspective not only threatened the way people might view Jesus' incarnation as a human — a central concept of Christianity that stresses the union of the spiritual and the physical worlds — it also threatened to unravel the concept of living in obedience to God. Think about it. Even today, someone might state (and some people in fact do): "If I have my spiritual loose ends wrapped up by believing in Jesus, I can now use my body to sin in any way I see fit!"

Did I mention this good-evil philosophy was quite a hit in the first century? Into this mess stepped the apostle John, confronting and combating this philosophy that had worked its way into the conventional wisdom of his times. Look at the dynamic approach John took. First, he actually used language and concepts familiar to his readers: a conflict exists between good and evil, light and darkness, God and the powers of this world. But — and this is a big but — John refused to say that all matter is evil. Instead, he stated that the good God created the world, Jesus became human, and Christians must stop sinning and live in obedience to God (a point he really hammers home later in his letter, 1 John). And in case anyone continued to insist that matter was evil, John punctuated his teaching by not only firmly maintaining that Jesus united spirit and matter (see John 1:14) but also clearly stating that the Holy Spirit will reside within all who believe (see John 14:15-17), uniting spirit and matter within every Christian.

These brief examples show how our context influences the ways we think about God and explain the gospel. Christianity doesn't exist apart from culture. John couldn't ignore it and neither can we. Just as Jesus lived on earth as a Jew who thought like a Jew, and just as the New Testament was written in Greek by people who thought in Greek categories, we're bound to read the Bible and practice our faith in our own cultures.

Understanding our cultural context helps us think about *how* we think. If we want to speak in relevant yet prophetic ways to our culture today, we need to follow the lead of Scripture's writers and take the next step of understanding our own culture today and how to work within its opportunities and challenges.

CULTURE'S OPPORTUNITIES AND CHALLENGES

"Wait," I asked with not a little panic. "Why is 'This Is the Day' the opening song for the worship service?"

"Oh, I really like that song," replied the worship pastor through his gently creased poker face. "It's a good way to lead off the service."

"I thought I told you that I can't stand that song," I replied. "My last church beat it to death. I don't know if I can go through with it."

During my days as a worship leader, I had a tendency to speak my mind. Actually, the only thing that's changed is that I'm not a worship leader anymore.

The pastors at my church were very accessible and willing to listen to comments or concerns, and even to personal vendettas against overplayed songs. They politely listened, worked through matters, and seemed to succeed in navigating their way through the maze of issues handed over to them, remaining firm when necessary. As the young, somewhat edgy worship leader, I probably gave them plenty of headaches, sleepless Saturday nights, and sweaty Sunday morning palms. Somehow, it all worked. I spoke my mind. They spoke theirs. We all listened. And the only disasters happened when I inevitably botched the hymn in the worship set.

When I told an Asian friend at seminary about one of the frank conversations I had with a pastor about changing the music of our church, he couldn't believe what he was hearing.[3]

"Did you really say that to your pastor?"

"Sure. Why not?"

"In our church, no one would just spout off like that. You have to respect your elders and your pastor."

"So if you feel like they're ignoring the younger generation or making a big mistake, you wouldn't have a meeting with your pastor about it?" I asked.

"It's hard to say. In the Asian church, we show our elders respect and don't attack the things they value. Still, it's hard to mix these values with the values picked up by the American-born children."

I was surprised to hear about this difference between our cultures. As Christians, we were both involved in ministry. But our cultures held different ways of showing respect, even in matters of Christian worship and congregational life. Begging to remove "This Is the Day" from the order of worship might work with some American pastors, but disgruntled youth in Asian churches need to take a very different course of action. By the way, in case you pity the poor worship pastor who had to put up with my whining about "This Is the Day," you'll be glad to know that he grinned widely after a silent moment and said, "Gotcha!" Yes, I'm outspoken *and* gullible—a horrible combination.

Of course, neither culture has a corner on respect for elders, but each culture will inevitably read the Bible through a different cultural lens. And both cultures present opportunities for sin. In extreme cases, the Asian approach could be used to ignore younger generations, while the American approach could be disrespectful to elders and leaders. This raises an important point about culture: Every culture has opportunities and challenges.

Throughout history, movements in culture have had both positive and negative effects on theology. And the same holds true today. We can more easily see these influences when we look back at historical events further removed from our own experiences. For example, the Protestant Reformation couldn't have happened in Europe without the cultural shift in philosophy that began valuing an individual's reasonable interpretation of the Bible[4] over the church's authority and traditions. This put the Bible in everyone's hands, a real benefit that we still enjoy. But relying on individual reason also fragmented the church as individual theologians began splitting from one another and creating a number of different denominations. In a world where the church and government had always been closely aligned, a divided church created all manner of political turmoil, as different nations adopted different denominations of Christianity and consequently attacked other nations that supported other denominations. This led to years of warfare and murder between Protestants and Catholics during the sixteenth and seventeenth centuries.[5] In other words, changes in the culture that led to relying on individual reason had both positive and negative effects on Christians and their beliefs about God.

EMBARKING ON THE LIFELONG JOURNEY

In much the same way, our thoughts about God today enjoy both opportunities and challenges because of our cultures. If we want to be culturally relevant yet hold on to the call to speak prophetically in our times, we need to enter into an ongoing conversation with culture. The bad news is that this conversation never ends, because our cultural values and beliefs are constantly shifting in one way or another. The good news is that we don't need to become experts overnight. We can begin the lifelong journey of simply paying attention to our surrounding culture and wrestling with the influences all around us that change how we understand God and live as disciples today.

An Ongoing Dialogue with Culture

When forming contextual theology—understanding God through the lens of a particular culture—I find it helpful to think of this ongoing process as a dialogue between that culture and the way God reveals himself in Scripture. Whether we admit it or not, our traditions and social structures interact with our study of the Bible. For example, I read the Bible as a white, middle-class, American male because that's who I am. If I have an awareness of my culture's particular perspective, I place myself in a better position to catch these influences on the way I interpret the Bible.

So if we're just typical Christians, how can we read the Bible with an awareness of our own cultural lens—both the good and bad parts? Fortunately, we don't need to cram lengthy academic books into our heads or sit through extended courses in culture. We can take our first steps into contextual theology simply by learning to look at our world and then to interpret it. In other words, we still go about our lives as before, but now we pay attention to the trends and messages in books, movies, newspapers, magazines, TV shows, and the people around us.

In chapter 5, we'll explore more specifically the culture we live in today. But for now, let's look at a few ways we can learn about culture and how we can remain relevant, learning to speak within our culture's categories, while also speaking to it prophetically as theologians who challenge the elements of culture opposed to God's revelation.

Think about our culture in America today. We're inundated with reality TV. We've seen the mixing of online videos, votes, and blogs with television and live events. To a large extent, we base our economic livelihood on consumer spending (often on products that we don't need). And we place a high value on individual financial independence. The average person can make all these observations. And if we dig into them a little deeper, asking what positive or negative values TV and movie characters portray or the ways blogs and online videos change public discourse, we can learn a great deal about who we are.

Of course, we have to admit that we're hitting just the tip of the iceberg. Still, these insights into who we are as a culture provide some clues about the lens we naturally use to read and interpret the Bible, as well as the issues we need to address prophetically in our society. For example, think about the cultural value of pursuing financial independence. We can see that verses such as Acts 2:44-45, which describe the earliest Christians' pooling their resources, will be tough to understand and apply. While not impossible, Americans will have more of an uphill battle digging into the meaning here than perhaps Christians in Mexican culture who place a high value on community and interdependence. We'll look more in depth at understanding who we are, how we see the world, and consequently how we read the Bible in chapters 4 through 8.

In the introduction of *Coffeehouse Theology*, I shared a brief sketch about American and Latin American theologies on God's blessing for the poor. This quick example hints at a way to challenge and hopefully overcome the limitations of our culture: learning from other people groups from history and from around the world. We need to do more than just be aware of the strengths and weaknesses of our own cultural lens. We also need to learn from Christians quite different from ourselves in order to test our understanding of God. We don't have to agree on everything, but, by testing our ideas, we can smoke out any flaws or limitations. If we want to run our beliefs about God through such a test, then we need to not only begin a dialogue with our own culture but with diverse cultures. That means possessing a willingness to learn from historic and global Christians, the topics of chapters 9 and 10, in order to broaden our understanding of God.

Dialogue That Transforms Culture

As we enter into a dialogue with culture so that we can evaluate our own cultural lens and broaden our perspectives, we can't simply try to be relevant and forget about our prophetic calling. In other words, we want to learn from culture, but at the same time we need to scrutinize it closely against the values of God in order to speak into the culture prophetically. For example, as Christians in America we might assume that God supports a policy of preemptive war, while Latin American Christians might believe that God supports a policy of revolution. Both face the challenge of comparing the values of their cultures against the values revealed in Scripture.

In addition to helping us understand how we view God, the goal of our ongoing dialogue with culture is faithfulness to God and bringing him into the cultures we interact with. We dialogue in order to find the good and the bad parts of culture; we learn from the good, but we should also work to transform the bad with the message and values of God. In fact, as God's representatives who bring his prophetic message, our dialogue with culture sometimes means we'll have to staunchly oppose its values and practices.

Perhaps you've heard of Dietrich Bonhoeffer, a Christian theologian in Germany in the 1930s and 1940s and a member of the resistance against Adolf Hitler. As Bonhoeffer evaluated the policies of the Nazi party, this otherwise peaceful man determined to oppose his country's government and policies. In the summer of 1944, Bonhoeffer was even linked to a group that attempted to assassinate Hitler. The bomb failed to kill Hitler, and countless German soldiers and civilians were rounded up, imprisoned, tortured, and executed for their ties to the plot. After his capture, Bonhoeffer spent several months in prison awaiting his trial while encouraging fellow believers. Even with the reality of the gallows looming in his mind, he boldly told the Gestapo that the Christian church was the sworn enemy of the Nazi cause. Bonhoeffer gave his captors additional evidence of his guilt by proclaiming his stance against the culture of his day, and he was eventually executed.

Bonhoeffer provides an extreme example of standing against a culture. While he was certainly concerned with transforming the culture of his day, he ultimately rejected it in order to remain faithful to Christ.

Many years before Bonhoeffer—and on the other side of the English Channel—William Wilberforce, a member of the British Parliament, was one of many who fought tirelessly for the abolition of slavery in England less than thirty years before the Civil War ravaged America. The movie *Amazing Grace* portrays the story of Wilberforce and his tireless fight of more than twenty years to end an institution that he and many other Christians deemed squarely at odds with the message of Scripture. Life could have been much easier if Wilberforce had simply followed along with the masses of his time. But as he interacted with the values and practices of his culture, he couldn't escape the need to fight against the slave trade, a battle he eventually won shortly before his death. As an ambassador for Christ in the political world of England, Wilberforce stood as a redemptive presence that helped transform English law and brought freedom to millions of slaves.

In his book *Adventures in Missing the Point*, Christian activist and theologian Tony Campolo offers a more recent example of prophetic action within culture. Desiring to help the impoverished people of the Dominican Republic, a group of Christian students bought stock in a major corporation that controlled a large portion of the country. At the annual meeting, the students challenged the stockholders to address problems that the company was spreading inside agriculture, education, health care, and the Dominican economy as a whole. Instead of being laughed out of the meeting, the students saw their challenge lead to sweeping changes within the company and in the Dominican Republic.

While we can't deny the immanent importance of sharing the gospel with individuals,[6] our relationship with Christ also calls us to challenge our culture's values with the freedom and new life of the gospel message. As theologian Lesslie Newbigin said, "[Jesus'] ministry entailed the calling of individual men and women to personal and costly discipleship, but at the same time it challenged the principalities and powers, the rulers of this world."[7]

NO LONGER WANDERING

Like the Palestinians I encountered on my trip to Bethlehem, every culture has its own assumptions and customs. If we want to be the messengers of Christ that he calls us to be, then we must understand the culture we're delivering his message to. Our culture reveals how we analyze information, communicate it, and view the world. So, if we want to step deeper into relationship with Christ and increase our commitment to reveal Christ to a world that desperately needs him, we must actively engage with culture.

In some ways, our cultural setting will enhance our relationship with Christ; in other ways it might serve more like a fence, keeping us from seeing a side of Christ we can't view from our particular place in the world. Interaction with our own culture and with other cultures around the world will provide tremendous insight into our own expression of Christianity and how it needs to either learn from or prophetically challenge the culture of our time. Only then can we take steps closer to God that we never before envisioned, create an awareness of potential pitfalls we previously couldn't see, and move into position to share the gospel in a relevant manner.

When we take our culture seriously, we won't find ourselves wandering aimlessly, hoping to find our way to God in the midst of so many confusing twists and turns in our world. Participating in contextual theology—learning about who we are, where we come from, and where we're going—advances our understanding of God and ensures that we end up where we need to be: living under the influence of God's truth.

▶ ▶ ▶ FOR FURTHER READING

- *Everyday Theology: How to Read Cultural Texts and Interpret Trends* (Grand Rapids, MI: Baker, 2007), edited by Kevin J. Vanhoozer
- *Models of Contextual Theology* (Maryknoll, NY: Orbis Books, 2002), by Stephen Bevans
- *Doing Local Theology: A Guide for Artisans of a New*

Humanity (Maryknoll, NY: Orbis Books, 2002), by Clemens Sedmak and Robert J. Schreiter

- *Foolishness to the Greeks: The Gospel and Western Culture* (Grand Rapids, MI: Eerdmans, 1986), by Lesslie Newbigin
- *Velvet Elvis: Repainting the Christian Faith* (Grand Rapids, MI: Zondervan, 2006), by Rob Bell
- *A Peculiar People: The Church as Culture in a Post-Christian Society* (Downers Grove, IL: InterVarsity, 1996), by Rodney Clap
- *Resident Aliens: Life in the Christian Colony* (Nashville: Abingdon, 1989), by Stanley Hauerwas and William H. Willimon
- *Faith Thinking: The Dynamics of Christian Theology* (Downers Grove, IL: InterVarsity, 2005), by Trevor Hart

For additional resources and discussion, see http://inamirrordimly .com/coffeehouse-theology/chapter-3.

A Web of Theology

This web illustrates the interconnected nature of Christian theology's sources and contexts.

Current chapter topic will be in bold.

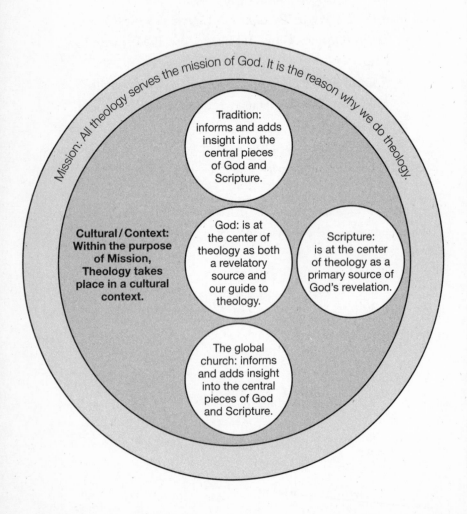

Mission: All theology serves the mission of God. It is the reason why we do theology.

Tradition: informs and adds insight into the central pieces of God and Scripture.

Cultural / Context: Within the purpose of Mission, Theology takes place in a cultural context.

God: is at the center of theology as both a revelatory source and our guide to theology.

Scripture: is at the center of theology as a primary source of God's revelation.

The global church: informs and adds insight into the central pieces of God and Scripture.

Chapter 4

THE MODERN WORLD

From The Two Towers to the Parking Lot

One of the most disconcerting feelings I've known swept through me as I left a stadium-seating theater showing of *The Two Towers*. I exited into a dark sea of asphalt, my car waiting at the far end of the mostly empty lot. Only moments before, a world of orcs, magic, walking trees, battles to the death, and sweeping cavalry charges had engulfed my mind. The silence, orderly white lines, and a few cars provided a striking contrast to the excitement of the movie, and it was a bit anticlimactic to start up my car without any fear of spells, avalanches, orcs, or arrows.

The few trees planted in my suburban desert stood quietly, generally keeping to themselves. The movie's portrayal of the final charge into the surging army of Saruman at Helm's Deep created an emotional high that left me craving more of Tolkien's world. Pushing my way through the honking swarms of cars on the suburban roads of Philadelphia left my soul and imagination feeling hollow, as if

I'd just pulled some nasty trick on them. At one moment the world seemed alive—trees attacked towers, magic influenced battles, and the people of earth allied themselves with either Saruman or Gandalf. And in the next moment I returned to my safe suburban haven where life is orderly, magicians are just illusionists, and the only invasion we think about is the threat of a stolen identity.

SUCKING THE MYTHS AND MAGIC OUT OF LIFE

Now imagine we lived in a world similar to Tolkien's land of magic, where unusual events in the heavens held supernatural significance: God controlled weather patterns, priests turned ordinary bread into the very body of Christ, diseases appeared and departed for unknown reasons, and the church infiltrated just about every area of life from the earthly government to the rules governing who escaped purgatory and who remained trapped. Your acts of penance might even help a long-dead relative enjoy a better life in heaven.

And let's imagine that, drawn out over the course of several hundred years, we see a gradual shift from this world—one alive with God and other supernatural forces—into another where people call into question and even replace many of these beliefs and values. The world of magic gets left behind for a new world that only believes what it can see.

If you can imagine this kind of shift, you have a glimpse of the changes that occurred in Western Europe from the Middle Ages (ACE 500–1500) to the modern age (ACE 1500–1970). A world that believed in God's direct intervention and looked to the supernatural to explain the events in everyday life gave way to a more scientific approach that valued proof and the wielding of orderly and rational thought.[1]

You might say that the modern age sucked a lot of the magic out of life.

A key word to keep in mind to describe the modern age is *reason*. Instead of relying on the princes, rulers, the church, or even looking to God to explain the world, people began to rely on their own ability to *reason* as they sorted through the matters of life. They began questioning political and church authorities who claimed a divine right to rule over them and to set up the laws of the land. And as people increasingly relied on reason to understand their world, they began to choose the findings of science, which seemed more objective and trustworthy. Ultimately, relying on reason to sort out all aspects of life led to the three big tenets of the modern age: universal truth, language with a clear meaning, and an orderly world.[2]

These three concepts — reliance on individual reason to uncover universal truth available to everyone, a direct correspondence between language and reality, and an orderly universe governed by laws — seem huge. But we'll explore the meaning of each in this chapter.

This modern age shaped much of the world we live in today, especially as the colonialism and imperialism of that time (primarily 1600–1900) exported western culture and business into continents such as Asia and Africa and carved up many of the countries we know today, including those in Africa and the Middle East. Christians played major roles during this shift from one age to another, and Christianity ended up looking very different as the modern age moved into full swing.

WHAT SHOULD THEOLOGIANS DO WITH HISTORY?

As we aim to do contextual theology, we need to consider these points from our historical past. Remember, contextual theology requires an understanding of who we are, how we think, and how we see the world. So we need to look at how the changes brought about by the modern era (also known as modernism) influence who we are today. We can't escape or ignore these influences because our current culture has either benefited from the modern age or been limited to the perspective of modern values and beliefs.

Here's a quick (and probably overly simplified) test: Do you believe that free-thinking citizens should be allowed to choose their leaders? If so, then you're likely a product of the modern age. However, this thinking affects more than just our politics. For example, we didn't start electing church leaders or "calling" our pastors *just* because we thought the process was biblical. We picked up the concepts from our times and applied it in a manner we saw as biblical.

Christians in the modern context typically see God through a modern lens. This has brought both benefits and problems to our thoughts about God. As our culture continues to respond to the influences of the modern era, understanding this period of history becomes increasingly critical. So let's break down some of the sweeping influences on how we think, who we are, and what we value.

First, we need to understand the values of the modern age—namely, the use of reason to find a world with universal truth, with clear language, and ordered by laws—and how it formed the world we have today. That's where we'll journey in this chapter.

Then, in chapter 5, we'll look at the shift from the modern era into a new context called postmodern. This era follows the modern age, and, while it offers some corrections to perceived shortfalls of the modern age, it also brings its own set of problems and challenges.

The payoff of our examination of modernism and postmodernism will come in chapter 6, where we'll discuss the ways these contexts influence Christian thinking. As we understand these cultural influences, we'll be better prepared to form contextual theology that's both relevant to the culture and prophetic to the parts of culture opposed to God.

As we start by exploring the modern age, keep in mind that we're capturing just a rough idea of this time period's contours—only the aspects that will provide the most help in our work of forming contextual theology. Let's start by looking at the "big picture" for this time and the formative events that brought it about.

SETTING UP THE MODERN WORLD

You could say that the shift from the Middle Ages to the modern era began in part with two scientists who spent most of their time shooting for the stars. Well, at least, these two—Nicolaus Copernicus and Galileo Galilei—spent a lot of time looking at the stars.

They really didn't discover anything all that new about the earth revolving around the sun. In fact, many astronomers in ancient India, Greece, and the Middle East had found a great deal of evidence for the centrality of the sun in our solar system. Still, because the Roman church wielded significant power over government, religion, and even science, European astronomers of the Middle Ages followed the church's lead by placing the earth in the center of the solar system with all heavenly bodies proceeding around it. The church backed up this claim with a solid assortment of Scripture passages portraying the earth as the *immovable* center of the solar system (see 1 Chronicles 16:30; Psalm 93:1; 96:10; 104:5). From Joshua's commanding the sun to stand still to the sun's racing from one horizon to the other in Ecclesiastes 1, biblical data pointed to an earth-centered solar system.

At the dawn of the sixteenth century, the Roman church had reached the height of its control over Europe. Immense wealth flowed in from rulers who feared excommunication while penitents gladly purchased indulgences for their own souls and the souls of their loved ones. This gave the church unquestioned power. However, trouble began to brew in regions of Poland and Germany and quickly spread across Europe, making the rest of the sixteenth century a particularly difficult time to be a leader in the church.

In 1514, astronomer Nicolaus Copernicus began to selectively circulate his theory that the earth revolved around the sun. This claim ran straight in the face of the church and, supposedly, the teachings of Scripture. Fortunately for the church at this point, Copernicus only laid the foundations for his theory, and he backed down from a confrontation with the church.

Shortly after Copernicus rattled the scientific and religious worlds, in 1517, a German monk named Martin Luther nailed his infamous *Ninety-Five Theses on the Power of Indulgences* to the door of the Wittenberg Castle Church, thereby kindling the Protestant Reformation. This movement had been brewing for years, but, aided by that relatively recent invention, the printing press, Luther's ideas enjoyed wide circulation, sparking debate among laity and clergy alike and forcing long-suppressed divisions in the church to shoot to the surface once more.

Matters became worse for the Roman church when Henry VIII of England formally separated from it in 1536.

In these three cases—Copernicus's theories about the center of the universe, Luther's spark under the Reformation, and Henry's withdrawal from the established church—individual thought won the day over the centralized authority of the church. This cleared room for the blow landed by Galileo Galilei.

Like Copernicus, Galileo didn't seek to attack or discredit the church when he advocated for the centrality of the sun. He simply took a different approach to biblical interpretation that allowed room for science and Scripture to coexist without contradiction. Galileo explained Scripture and science as two truths that could never contradict one another. Science observes the mechanics of our world, while

Scripture explains what people observe. So while the mechanics of the universe show that the earth revolves around the sun, people on earth see that the sun *appears* to be orbiting the earth as the sun moves from one horizon to the other.[3] In more general terms, the writers of the Bible made accurate observations about physical events, but they weren't setting out to determine the scientific process behind these events.

Although Galileo enjoyed periods of popularity with both church and public, from 1616 to 1642, the Roman church attacked him and eventually prohibited him from circulating his ideas. With the Protestant Reformation in full swing, the Roman church began to doubly assert its authority in matters of heresy—both perceived and real. Consequently, in 1633, the church banned Galileo's *Dialogue Concerning the Two Chief World Systems* that presented his sun-centered theory in layman's terms. In addition, he was commanded to make a public renunciation and condemned to indefinite house arrest. Obedient to the church rather than science, Galileo presented a statement cursing and detesting his heresy regarding the universe. He spent the remainder of his life imprisoned in a secluded house outside of Florence. Even with this devastating verdict weighing down on him, Galileo persisted in his wonder at the natural world and managed to write yet another book that was smuggled out, published, and eventually contributed to the theory of universal gravitation.[4]

In 1758, the Roman church finally lifted all bans from Galileo's work, but the damage had been done. In a case pitting church authority and Scripture against science, cool and objective science guided by human reason clearly arrived at the correct conclusions. Europe would never be the same.[5] People no longer accepted the Roman church and secular rulers as divine appointments able to rule the "ignorant" masses. The focus of modern thought shifted to the power of individuals who could read and rationalize on their own. Science and other academic disciplines began to blossom, giving rise to a period known as the Enlightenment, a term closely linked with modernism. A major tenet of the Enlightenment asserted that each person should use reason to interact with the world. Simply taking an authority's word was no longer good enough.

MODERNISM IN A NUTSHELL

René Descartes (1596–1650), the renowned philosopher who arrived at the maxim "I think, therefore I am," distinguished himself as one of the definitive figures in the founding of philosophical modernism. With this statement expressing his doubt about everything around him *except his own ability to think*, Descartes sought to attain a certainty in knowledge that equaled the certainty achieved in mathematics or geometry.[6] In other words, Descartes advocated clearing away everything you've ever known and beginning any study with a blank slate, letting your own observations fill in the void with pure truth. Believing that prejudice and preconceived notions weighed down knowledge, Descartes relied on what he called "radical doubt" to clear away these obstacles to pure knowledge.[7]

This method actually hearkened back to Greek philosophy—rediscovered during Descartes' era thanks to the printing press—and it set the course for the modern age. Descartes' philosophy elevated reason as the primary analytical tool and ruled out faith as a driving force in the pursuit of knowledge.[8] This quest for pure and universal knowledge applied a rigorous method of doubt so that every belief could be constructed on a certain foundation. With the proper methods in the hands of reason, modern philosophers sought to grasp the absolute or universal truth that would apply to all people at all times.

Descartes hit the scene in Europe during the Thirty Years War (1618–1648), a conflict that decimated the continent. In central Europe, Protestants came under continual attack by Catholic rulers who dreamed of reuniting Europe under the Roman church. Protestants and Catholics took sides and fought a series of battles won by the Catholics, resulting in the brutal oppression of Protestants. Alarmed at the fate of their Protestant brethren, the Danes renewed the conflict in 1625 but suffered defeat and were forced to withdraw. Finally, after the Danes exited, the Protestant ruler of Sweden won a decisive victory over the Catholic forces. In the meantime, France joined the Swedes in plundering Catholic territories in Central Europe, which led to further bloodshed and chaos.

Historians estimate that the Thirty Years War reduced the population of the German territories from 21 million to 13 million, not to mention the toll taken on the countryside and the cities devastated by the amassed artillery of the growing European armies. Because of the sheer horror brought by this war and the millions of lives it claimed, the best and brightest minds began searching for ways to understand the world, to attain certain knowledge, and to avoid the senseless brutality of war. This was the world of René Descartes, and it was more than ready to welcome his new theories about human thought.

To a continent ravaged by the Thirty Years War, the hope of a uniform method of attaining certainty indeed came as good news.[9] European thinkers hoped to use the power of reason to resolve their differences and attain a universal story (also known as a metanarrative) to unite the world under one perspective. [10] If multiple perspectives caused so much war and destruction, then an objective view that all could attain would act as a pressure-release valve the continent so badly needed.

Of course, with the rise of reason and the scientific method, people began to rule out religious experiences with the divine until they could be proven through testing. Theologian Stanley Grenz notes, "Enlightenment thinkers began to appeal to human reason rather than externally imposed revelation as the final arbiter of truth. In fact, they appealed to reason in order to determine what constitutes revelation."[11]

The revolution kindled by Descartes filtered down into every academic discipline and began to completely reshape European thinking. The tenets of the medieval world gave way to these new Enlightenment principles:

- *Reason:* The world can be understood through disciplined and rational observation.
- *Natural law:* The universe is orderly and governed by laws.
- *Autonomy:* Individuals are able to test the external claims of all authorities.
- *Harmony:* The universe has an overarching order; it is inherently reasonable.
- *Progress:* Because the universe is both orderly and knowable, the use of the proper methods can lead to true knowledge.[12]

People eventually stopped viewing the world as God's revelation and instead saw the world as more of a machine governed by laws, such as gravity or the laws of thermodynamics. *Individuals* were expected to make decisions for themselves regarding their beliefs. Scientists vigorously pursued the mastery of the world, expecting to manipulate nature at will. And the human mind was considered capable of perceiving the world with complete objectivity.

MODERNITY'S THREE ARENAS OF INFLUENCE[13]

As we zoom in on this modern landscape, we need to look at three areas uniquely formed by this period of history: what we can know (epistemology), what we can say (language), and the nature of our world (metaphysics).

Keep in mind that these three areas are simply points on the much larger map of modernism. If I know where to find Philadelphia as a dot on a map, I know a few things about it. It's close to water and, due to its eastern location, I can guess that it was among the earlier American settlements. However, Philadelphia consists of a lot more than what fits on a map. Thick guidebooks, works of history, and every other kind of book provide details of the city for those interested in learning more. In the same way, even if we touch on a few features of modernism here, we shouldn't confuse my limited map with a comprehensive guide book or a trip to South Philly for a cheesesteak at Pat's or Geno's.

Still, we need to start somewhere, and these three points of modernism will serve us well.[14] This simple map of the modern world will help us recognize some of the influences on our thinking today, and especially the philosophy that gave rise to the world we do theology in today. As we seek to understand God, we need to keep these world-shaping areas of modernism in mind because they shaped the Christians who handed down our doctrines about God and how we relate God to our culture. A look at this backdrop for our world reminds us that so much of what we believe is a reaction to another time in history and that future generations will most likely devise new ways of thinking that react to our current culture.

What We Can Know

How would you respond if I told you a magician stopped a snowstorm in my town so I could make it to a doctor's appointment? You probably wouldn't believe me. After all, you've learned to doubt such supernatural events. There's no way to test my claim about the magician, and you happen to know from the weather report that a front swept in from the north and cleared the skies. So you could claim that magicians don't exist, that my claim can't be verified, and that science offers a perfectly reasonable explanation.

Did you catch the word *reasonable* in there?

In the modern age, people learned to use reason to get at absolute certainty about any subject or issue. We might define *absolute certainty* as knowledge beyond the shadow of any doubt. Of course, the world wasn't inherently unreasonable before the modern age. People still demanded evidence. The difference is one of degree.

Because Christianity relies on faith in order to accept supernatural events that can't be demonstrated with critical observation, we can see how the modern era's desire for absolutely certain knowledge wreaked havoc with our beliefs. How in the world could a Christian prove to a scientist that Jesus is really the Son of God?

While thinkers in the modern age doubted plenty, they did believe that science would lead them to pure knowledge. They believed that principles extracted from the grimy confines of everyday life could ultimately be set up as absolute truth that stands at all times for all people. This absolute truth dominated thinking to the degree that if two people committed to finding the truth disagreed on their findings, they believed the fault resided in the integrity of the thinkers' methods. In a world where thinkers sought to erase all doubt and achieve a god-like perspective of reality that rose above the limits of a particular culture or place in time, uncertainty became the enemy and absolutes took center stage.[15]

Of course, Christians during the modern age faced daunting challenges as they tried to present a religion of faith to a world that simply refused to accept unreasonable doctrines that link God with the world. Remember Galileo? His predicament shows the tension between science and religion that marked the modern age, as many people eventually shut out God from the pure knowledge that could be demonstrated and tested by science.

What We Can Say
"It is what it is."

New Englanders use this little homespun phrase all the time. I think it's another way of saying, "Go with the flow," a kind of fatalism that seems to insinuate, "Take what you've got, shut up, and stop thinking about it."

One day, a plumber came to our home to give us an estimate on a water softener for our well. He took a few tests, whistled, and then told us that we needed a $3,000 system to balance the acidity in our water that somehow related to our pipes bursting.

"Yeah, these wells can be a real pain, but ya know, it is what it is."

After just purchasing and renovating our home, we didn't have $3,000 lying around. So we decided to take our chances with the pipes bursting. I stuffed the plumber's estimate somewhere in my filing cabinet never to be seen again.

It is what it is.

If I can add a slight twist to this New England quip, the modern age approached language in much the same way. In the modern era, words were what they were—no more, no less. If thinkers in the modern age pursued certain knowledge that couldn't be doubted at any time or place, then we should expect the same people to think of language as a clear representation of reality. They said what they meant and meant what they said. And what they said meant something very specific. When only one true interpretation exists, who needs ambiguity or additional explanations? It is what it is.

Modern thinkers believed we can communicate in such a way that our words reflect reality precisely. Further, the modern view of language's holding a one-to-one correspondence with reality wasn't limited to verbal communication. Interpretation of the printed word also fell into line with modernism. If words have exactly one correspondence to reality, then the possibility of multiple interpretations can't exist. So, people studied works of literature with the intent of finding the one meaning of a story.

As a result of this correlation between language and reality, Christians in the modern age used reason and a rather scientific approach to study Scripture with the goal of tapping into the "plain meaning" of the text. As Christians read the Bible, searching for one clear meaning and timeless absolutes, something odd began to happen. Although many Christians studied the Bible for themselves in the noble pursuit of God's truth, Protestants experienced periods of tension among fellow believers and continued to fragment and divide.

The Nature of Our World

The story of Aladdin has found its way into the lore of many cultures around the world. After all, who wouldn't want a genie able to provide three wishes?

But why stop at three?

What would happen if Aladdin figured out how the genie fulfilled his wishes and then determined a way to manipulate the lamp so that he could fulfill every desire without the genie's help? In other words, what if Aladdin got rid of the genie and found a way to make the lamp work for him? The result would be no genie and no limits.

In many ways, if you can bear with me, the modern age essentially kicked the genie out of the lamp and used the lamp for its own purposes — except the genie represents God and the lamp represents our world.

With the elevation of science and the reason of individuals above the authority of the church, a new view of the universe emerged without God (or a genie). Instead of seeing the world as God's creation shrouded in mystery—to some degree during the Middle Ages, people viewed droughts, comets, earthquakes, and other disasters as supernatural phenomena—science stepped in and revealed the natural causes behind these events. As philosophy professors Steven Best and Douglas Kellner emphasize:

> In the new scientific interpretation, nature was governed by laws that could be apprehended through reason and experimental methods. . . . The goal of knowledge shifted from contemplating a divinely organized, living universe to conquering and mastering dead nature, a universe reduced to mere matter-in-motion, a storehouse of raw materials for human use.[16]

In other words, modern philosophy described the universe as mechanistic, functioning within the bounds of laws and other discernable cycles. If all mystery, divinity, and subjectivity could be removed, the Enlightenment's quest for certainty could be fulfilled, removing the free radical of divine intervention from the works of objective observation. What's more, once people got a grasp on nature's system, they could essentially become its master and utilize it for their own purposes. And if the universe operates within a set system of rules, then miracles and other manifestations of the divine can be explained away.

Under the influence of modernism, explorers set sail from Europe to find new lands, leading to the colonization of "new worlds" that were inhabited by native peoples. Nearly every European country was engaged in a race to colonize, imposing their universally applicable absolute truths and laws on the natives who were deemed uncivilized because of their inability to rise above their supposed cultural preferences and superstitions to accept the super-culture and universal truths of the Europeans. Western nations also busied themselves using the resources of these new lands to boost their economies. As the world's status was downgraded from creation of God to machine, humanity had the impetus to mine the land for jewels, fuels, and other commodities. Coal and fossil fuels were then used to power the industrial revolution, pouring pollutants into the atmosphere and setting the stage for the conveniences and challenges of modern civilization. These choices and policies have created some of the conflicts and changes in climate that continue to challenge us today.

On the other hand, there were incredible advances made during the modern era in medicine, medical procedures, biology, physics, and chemistry by relying on these scientific laws. Vaccines put a halt to deadly diseases that had previously plagued Europe. While modernity's characterization of the world as an orderly machine perpetrated many of humanity's abuses of the world, it brought its share of benefits. Even if our world is quite different, it has certainly improved in many concrete ways.

The response of Christians to the "world as machine" perspective in the modern age was mixed. Some groups (many liberal or mainline denominations) embraced the move of science away from the supernatural, gave up on the miracles and other supernatural elements of Scripture, and changed Christianity into a movement for the betterment of society. Others (many conservative Protestant denominations) held on to the supernatural influence of God while trying to understand God in the terms of laws and essential truths. They used the tools of science to explain God, even offering proofs for the existence of God. Still others (such as Roman Catholics) reformed their church through major councils, but still nurtured the mystical and spiritual elements of their faith—especially in the practice of center-ing prayer and the liturgy of the Eucharist. As thinkers described the world as orderly and governed by laws, Christians did their best to adapt, explaining their faith anew in the midst of changing times.

WHERE THE MODERN AGE LEAVES US

While matters could have been worse, the modern age presented many challenges to the world and especially to Christians of that era. Sincere and well-meaning philosophers, fed up with the turmoil of warfare in the midst of political instability and religious division, did their best to recast the world through the lens of reason. While they didn't necessarily set out to supplant the church, they ended up removing religious explanations for the world and replacing them with the cool logic of science and reason.

The modern age's reliance on reason dramatically changed the direction and makeup of the world. Individualism took hold, nation-states rose with free elections, thinkers attempted to overcome all doubt and uncertainty, and Europe began to export its Enlightenment culture all over the globe in exchange for tea, sugar, and slaves. In this context, Christians had to figure out a way to communicate truth, present faith in the best light possible, and eventually combat the unjust exploitation and neglect of the poor in their own countries and in some cases around the world.

In addition, certain thinkers began to rebel, recognizing the flaws in the ways they pursued knowledge in the modern age. They began collecting diverse perspectives on truth. Students of language realized that a variety of interpretations can exist for what is said and written—that language is a fairly uncertain entity that might not correspond as closely to reality as they believed. And then scien-tists discovered that some of their laws weren't as reliable as once thought. The world holds a lot more complexity and mystery than they suspected. Even if they couldn't bring God into the laboratory, they began to see holes where something or someone else could fit.

To top it off, although everyone has and uses reason, many people began reacting against the modern age's *complete* reliance on reason to arrive at truth. They saw reason as necessary, yet in concert with a variety of additional factors that contribute to what constitutes the truth.

So what happened? Unable to answer new questions and data constantly coming in, the modern age essentially ran out of gas. As modernism stepped aside, a new philosophy took hold that critiqued the modern age and tried to correct its flaws. Because it arose "after" modernism, beginning in the 1970s, this new philosophy confronting Christian theology is commonly known as postmodernism.

As we move into the postmodern era, we may find that though we don't have genies we can rub out of lamps, there still is mystery and even "magic" in the world after all.

▶ ▶ ▶ FOR FURTHER READING

- *The Creators: A History of Heroes of the Imagination* (New York: Vintage, 1993), by Daniel Boorstin
- *The Discoverers: A History of Man's Search to Know His World and Himself* (New York: Phoenix, 2001), by Daniel Boorstin
- *The Reformation: A History* (New York: Penguin, 2005), by Diarmaid MacCulloch
- *Reform and Conflict: From the Medieval World to the Wars of Religion* (Grand Rapids, MI: Baker, 2005), by Rudolph W. Heinze
- *The Age of Reason: From the Wars of Religion to the French Revolution* (Grand Rapids, MI: Baker, 2006), by Meic Pearse

- *Introduction to Philosophy: A Christian Perspective* (Grand Rapids, MI: Baker, 1987), by Norman L. Geisler and Paul D. Feinberg

For additional resources and discussion, see http://inamirrordimly .com/coffeehouse-theology/chapter-4.

A Web of Theology

This web illustrates the interconnected nature of
Christian theology's sources and contexts.

Current chapter topic will be in bold.

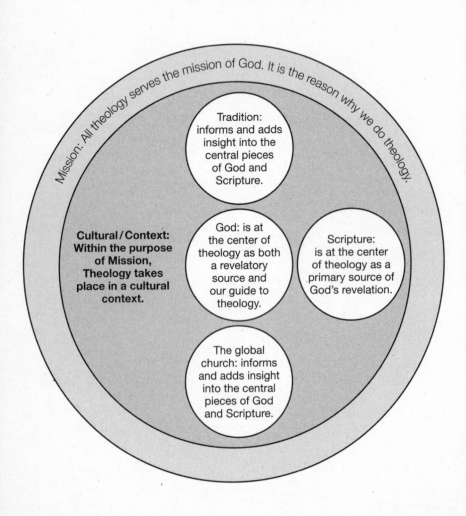

Mission: All theology serves the mission of God. It is the reason why we do theology.

**Cultural/Context:
Within the purpose
of Mission,
Theology takes
place in a cultural
context.**

Tradition:
informs and adds
insight into the
central pieces
of God and
Scripture.

God: is at
the center of
theology as both
a revelatory
source and
our guide to
theology.

Scripture:
is at the center
of theology as a
primary source of
God's revelation.

The global
church: informs
and adds insight
into the central
pieces of God
and Scripture.

Chapter 5

THE POSTMODERN AGE

Andy Griffith Meets *The Real World*

I really don't like a certain nationwide moving company. Even if I don't tell you which one I'm talking about, you can probably guess—especially if they've ruined one of your moves.

First, when Julie and I moved from the Philadelphia area to Vermont, this company lost our reservation. When the truck we rented broke down, they left us stranded on the side of the road for eight hours before we decided to turn in to a hotel for the night. They promised to reimburse us for all of our hotel expenses, but they didn't. Again and again, they refused to reimburse us for our broken-down rental. When I called to try to sort out the situation, they grew increasingly abusive toward me on the phone. After putting up with this for four months, I was ready to hit back—which I admit probably wasn't the best idea.

While I blogged the details of our trial and saved friends from a similar fate, the knockout punch, coup de grace, and all-around revenge had to do with the consumer reports segment on a local newscast. I submitted my story and was delighted when they contacted me.

As part of the story, the reporter took several of this company's trucks for inspection and some of them failed. He interviewed other couples with horror stories and then arrived to interview us. I had my story together: The company has a broken system that leaves customers stranded and in dangerous circumstances. While that served as a good line for his purposes, the reporter wanted something a little more . . . emotional. During the interview, he asked questions such as, "How angry does this make you feel?"

What was I supposed to say? *"Well perhaps* perturbed *is a better word for my emotional state at the moment."*

I thought the point of the story was rather cut-and-dried. But I saw firsthand that reporters often put their own angle on stories. They might even stack the deck to make sure the "facts" point in the right direction and move in the proper order. In this case, I certainly was angry about our experience with the moving company. But the reporter asked questions to elicit certain responses that we weren't necessarily feeling on our own.

After this experience, it struck me how this reporter's desire to slant his story a particular way reveals how our culture perceives "truth" and "facts." Rather than being an objective observer who fairly presented all of the facts of our story, the reporter showed that we all have an angle on the truth, we all have a version of the story to tell. As we've moved beyond the modern age and into what philosophers and sociologists call the postmodern era, we've replaced the desire to seek out one story or perspective leading to one large and all-encompassing truth. In the place of the one perspective, we're learning to consider and value a diversity of perspectives—a collection of smaller, localized truths that grow out of our own observations.

TRICKLE-DOWN PHILOSOPHY

When you hear the word *postmodern*, what do you think it means? Maybe even more importantly, do you care about postmodernism? Do we really need to understand this word in order to talk about Jesus today?

The answer to this last question is yes and no. Postmodernism is the current cultural lens that we see God through, so we do need to understand it. This philosophy touches how we think, how we make decisions, how we read and interpret the Bible, and how we determine truth. However, understanding the influence of postmodernism on our world and theology isn't the same as saying we need to master *all* that this word brings with it. Because our goal is to do contextual theology, we'll study God with an awareness of our world, not necessarily a complete mastery.

So what is postmodernism? This word typically refers to a period of time following the modern age, a new era marked by an interest in finding new perspectives to describe our world. Instead of seeking out one perspective that leads to one large, all-encompassing truth, thinkers began to seek smaller truths by embracing the complexity, chaos, and diversity of the world.

Even if you've never heard the word *postmodern* before, I guarantee that you've personally seen, experienced, and even participated in its influences. In the United States, our society has become thoroughly postmodern in its practice and thinking, even though few of us actually know what exactly to call these changes. Big shifts in philosophy have a way of trickling slowly through society, gradually changing our world until we wonder what hit us.[1] For example, Christians in America might wonder why new age and eastern religions began to catch on in the 1970s—a trend that continues in popular culture with yoga and the practices of meditation and centering. We might also question why many in our culture mock claims about salvation through Christ alone, or why fewer and fewer young adults find the Christian faith relevant.[2] At least in part, these problems grow out of a change in thinking caused at its roots by postmodernism.[3]

A POSTMODERN ROADMAP

In Chapter 4, we talked about a map of Philadelphia with roads and dots that tell us enough to find our way around, yet the map doesn't provide the extensive and technical details of a guidebook. As we explore postmodernism, we'll learn enough to find our way around using our map, but we won't necessarily master a philosophy guidebook.

And this start is plenty. We want to learn about our culture so that we can remain aware of its influence on our theology, but we don't have to be culture experts. We're not setting out to master postmodernism as a philosophical concept. Instead—much like our sketch of the modern age—we want to gain a broad understanding of how postmodernism changes our world. Then we can spot its influences in our culture and in how we do theology and relate it to our culture. Our goal is to avoid mixing the values of God with the values of our culture—a practice known as syncretism. Further, we also want to understand ways we can meaningfully bring God to our culture, so we can speak with relevance on points of agreement and prophetically on points of disagreement.

In order to look at some of the contours of the shift from modern to postmodern, let's enter a fictional clash between two TV shows that represent the modern and postmodern eras, respectively: *The Andy Griffith Show* and *The Real World*. We'll then use points in the story as illustrations to find what we need to know about postmodernism and its influence as we do contextual theology.

FROM MAYBERRY TO THE REAL WORLD

Andy Taylor, sheriff of Mayberry, glared at the three young adults seated across from him. With fists clenched, Deputy Barney Fife stood across the room near the jail cells. The three young people shifted and squirmed. One sat on his hands, another dug her fists into her pockets, while the third — a smooth-cheeked young man — sniffed, whimpered, and dabbed at his moist eyes.

"Now let's get this matter ironed out," Sheriff Taylor demanded. "You three upset a bunch of people today. For the record, let's get your names."

Folding his hands under his arms, the first young man replied, "Tom Stivers."

The young woman said, "Julia Durow."

Pulling himself together, the other young man shuddered slightly and said, "Drew Smith."

"Would one of you like to be the spokesman for the group?" asked the sheriff.

They looked at each other. Julia's face remained solid stone, with only her shoulders rising slightly. Drew wiped at one eye and nodded weakly toward Tom. He nodded back and then turned toward Andy. "I'll speak for the group," Tom said.

"Okay then. Barney reportedly found you three trespassing on land belonging to four different people. Do you agree with that report?"

"What do you mean when you say 'trespassing'?"

Andy paused, stirred his coffee, and looked up at Tom again. Tom wasn't smirking or smiling. "Well, I mean wrongfully entering another person's property."

"Is walking wrong?"

"Uh, no, it isn't, but we received four different phone calls from folks saying that you were walking right through their backyards. People are quiet and private around here. They don't take trespassing lightly."

"I didn't see any signs posted in those fields you're calling their backyards. How could we have known? Besides, we didn't damage anyone's property. I think you need to redefine *trespassing*."

"Were you or were you not on someone else's land?"

"How can someone actually own land? Aren't we really all trespassing to a certain degree?"

"I don't follow you. Look, I need to wrap up this investigation, and it seems awfully clear to me that you three are guilty."

Julia let out a sigh, while Drew wiped at his eyes again. Quietly, he whined to himself, "I'll never get into college with a criminal record."

Then Tom leaned forward, his eyes narrowing sharply to meet Andy's glare. "There's another way to do this," he said. "You think you can explain everything with tidy definitions, always arriving at a clear right and wrong."

"Well, of course," replied Andy.

"But life isn't like that. In some towns and countries, it's perfectly permissible to walk on someone else's land provided no damage is done. How were we supposed to know that you define trespassing differently here?"

Andy snapped back, "There's a right, and there's a wrong. Stop trying to muddy the waters here."

"I'm not muddying the waters. That's what you're doing. Listen, do you have a small room we could use for a minute?"

"I don't see how that relates to anything," Andy said.

"Humor me," Tom said. "Drew, I think you should be the first one in the confessional room."

Andy sighed and tilted his head to look across the room. "Barney, let them use that side office."

Shaking his head, Barney opened the office door. A cameraman appeared from a dark corner of the jailhouse and followed Drew into the room, giving Barney a start. Andy and Barney watched as Drew dug a small comb into his neatly arrayed hair. The cameraman set up a microphone in front of him.

After counting down, the cameraman gave Drew the action sign. He took a deep breath and then began to share, "I've been backpacking all over Europe, and the people there let you walk just about wherever you want. There's no such thing as trespassing unless someone posts a sign. The people in this town don't seem to understand how trespassing works. Besides, I would never risk arrest by knowingly breaking the law. A criminal record wouldn't look good on my college application."

Drew relaxed into his chair, and the cameraman gave the all-clear signal. Andy and Barney looked on with wide eyes.

"How about going next Barney?" said Tom.

"Why? I mean, what are you doing?" asked the startled deputy.

"This is the confessional room. We each share our side. It's a better way of getting to the truth. Why would we only listen to one person?"

"Okay, who's next?" the cameraman said as he stepped in. "Barney?"

Barney leaned close to Andy, who tilted his head toward his deputy.

"Andy," he said, "I've got a bad feeling about this crew. They could change Mayberry forever. How about we just let them go?"

"I think you're right," Andy replied. "Besides, I don't want to enter that confessional room without a script to follow."

NOW LEAVING MAYBERRY

Comparing *The Andy Griffith Show* with *The Real World* is just one of many comparisons we could make when discussing the shift from modernism to postmodernism.[4] The world of Mayberry—with an objective authority figure using reason to sort out matters, a closely followed and orderly script, and largely black and white values—embodies modernism. On the other hand, postmodern values scream through *The Real World* with its uneasy equality given to different perspectives, unscripted and chaotic interaction among the characters, and a mishmash of moral observations throughout the show.

People can't help being stuck in a particular time and place. The shared symbols, values, and words of a particular group provide the keys to how the people in that group communicate, interpret, and assign meaning. Andy Taylor, sheriff of Mayberry, inhabits a modern world where citizens expected the trusted authority figures to call the shots and interpret reality for everyone else. Tom challenges this world by providing a postmodern perspective where leaders collaborate and utilize the shared viewpoints of others.

Keep in mind that neither approach is more correct than the other. Both have weaknesses and strengths. But one has become more relevant and natural for today's world, and that's what concerns us. So unless we consider reruns of *The Andy Griffith Show* a sufficient litmus test for determining cultural trends, we have to admit that our world has moved away from modernism and into postmodernism. Let's look briefly at how we got to this point.

THE POSTMODERN UPHEAVAL

In the twentieth century, modern philosophy fell to pieces after World War I and World War II and during the tensions of the Cold

War. Amid this chaos and complexity, the objectivity and understanding provided by reason and the scientific method appeared to fail humanity. Doubts arose over the possibility of universal laws and absolutes that govern morality and understanding. Language seemed less clear cut. And the collision of global cultures revealed a wider spectrum of diversity than modern thinkers could ever imagine.

As colonies around the world found their own voices, they challenged the stories and values imposed by western powers and began to fight for their own control. Many of these territories won their independence in the years following World War II.

In spite of the advances modernity brought to society, philosophers began to critique its shortfalls. These thinkers embraced the diversity and complexity of the world, ushering in the postmodern age. If *reason* summarized the modern age, *diversity* helps us catch many of the values of postmodern times.

Postmodernism began to appear in the architecture of the 1920s. Later, during the 1960s and 1970s, the philosophy caught on in universities, especially within literary studies. For example, women began to question the long-held interpretations of men, bringing their own values and insights to their study of literature and arriving at different readings of texts. Soon literary interpretations emerged that celebrated the unique perspective of women, and there was an increase in the study of African American, Latin American, and other minorities' works.

Growth of postmodern thinking in this area certainly held implications for Christians reading the Bible.[5] In the wake of these changes in literary studies, Western theologians and philosophers needed to re-examine the dominant interpretations of Scripture by learning about the views of Christians from outside the West.

Related to diversity, the distinguishing mark of the postmodern age is its rejection of a universal story or metanarrative to explain the order of the entire world. As pastor and theologian Brian McLaren notes, with the abuses of totalitarian dictators fresh in their minds, postmodern thinkers believe that "*metanarrative* implies domination, coercion, eradication of opponents, imposition of beliefs or behaviors on minorities against their will."[6] Instead of one grand story that all members of humanity go along with, postmodern thinkers place a greater emphasis on the diversity of perspectives present in the world.[7]

Our fictional scenario in the town of Mayberry illustrates this tension between the modern and postmodern worlds, when Tom advocates for a more complex and communal understanding of truth that considers the slippery nature of language and local nature of laws. We can also look to the documentaries *Bowling for Columbine*, *Fahrenheit 9/11*, and *Sicko* by filmmaker Michael Moore for another clue that our world no longer places a single perspective on the same pedestal as modernity did. Moore blurred the boundary between reporting news and providing entertainment by reporting on "facts" from an unapologetically liberal perspective. In addition, the Internet and its ability to instantly connect a variety of cultures make the value of multiple perspectives increasingly apparent. With this form of communication, we can easily learn what people in Iran think about American foreign policy or what the church in Africa believes.

As Christians, we find ourselves in this strange postmodern world with opportunities to speak with relevance yet with the threat of mixing the values of God with the values of culture (syncretism). Our challenge is to create a meaningful dialogue with postmodernism that uncovers the parts of the culture that connect well with the values of God, while also discovering the aspects of the culture that we need to oppose and even work to change to fulfill our prophetic calling.

Certainly we can use certain aspects of postmodern thinking. For example, some stories in the Bible champion the underdog, and

100

the diversity of postmodernism takes note of underdogs, not just favorites. However, the postmodern call for a diversity of perspectives without a commitment to some measure of truth can pose a real problem for Christians, who believe that God uses Scripture to teach truth and to lead us into belief. We need to carefully juggle these kinds of challenges as we seek to form contextual theology that is both relevant and prophetic.

NAVIGATING THE HAZARDS OF POSTMODERNISM

On one hand, the emphasis on valuing diverse perspectives seems to be a very appealing approach, enhancing our view of the world with the insights of other contexts. However, some people fear this development; if we value diversity, we might simply spend our time appreciating the contributions of others without evaluating them. After all, should we question the merits of what others think? Or should we act like we're attending an exhibition of elementary school art, where we look for the best in everyone's work: "Wow, you really like to use a lot of colors when you scribble!" In addition, if we take valuing diverse perspectives too far, will we lose all sense of order and simply end up with a hodgepodge of ideas and opinions? What's more, if we don't think our own perspective is adequate, then what's to stop us from buying into wholesale relativism where everyone appears to be right?

To counter these dangers, Christians in postmodern culture can agree that truth is complex and hard to completely understand. Yet we can also reject the belief of some postmodern thinkers that truth is unattainable. Christians can also agree that we'll never overcome doubt completely. After all, Christians rely on faith, and we can focus and sharpen the truth of our faith when we bring it into contact with other views. For example, the postmodern perspective actually strengthens the doctrine of Christ's divinity, because it has stood throughout all of church history even in the midst of heated debate and division in the early church, and because every cultural expression of Christianity from around the world affirms it.

On the other hand, issues such as the abolition of slavery and women's suffrage give us reasons for caution and humility in our thinking, because Bible-believing Christians at one time actually advocated against these movements. Today, we shake our heads in disbelief. Yet we can look at how the cultures of these Christians had a significant influence on how they viewed passages in Scripture about women and slavery to arrive at views we'd never accept today.

In other words, while we can rely on many central doctrines of Christianity that have been in place for years, we also need to learn from our history that sometimes we don't have the complete picture. As we seek historic and global perspectives on doctrinal issues, we can get a better handle on the truth, as long as we commit ourselves to finding it and don't give in to a disordered mix of ideas. Perhaps postmodernism truly takes the apostle Paul's words into account: "Now we see but a poor reflection as in a mirror; then we shall see face to face. Now I know in part; then I shall know fully, even as I am fully known" (1 Corinthians 13:12).

As a Christian, I can comfortably say that I believe in truth. But I know I don't have access to *all* of it. That belongs to God alone. If I'm talking with an atheist, and I claim that Jesus is the Son of God, I can't prove it scientifically beyond the shadow of a doubt. As Christians in the postmodern context, we might have a great advantage over our modern counterparts, because we can simply admit that our beliefs lack conclusive and scientifically verifiable proof, yet we can remain solid in our convictions because we have the witness of believers around the world, tradition, and Scripture.[8] Faith *must* enter the equation when we talk about God, because without faith we can't please God (see Hebrews 11:6).

With these basic understandings and hopes of how Christians can survive and thrive in a postmodern context, let's look at the same three categories we examined when reviewing the modern worldview in chapter 4. In addition, we'll explore how our current postmodern culture has changed these three areas: what we can know, what we can say, and the nature of our world.

What We Can Know

Remember, in the modern age, "what we can know" represented the idea of people using reason to get at absolute certainty about any subject or issue. We defined absolute certainty as knowledge beyond the shadow of any doubt. In the modern age, many thinkers worked on building their knowledge from the ground up, arranging the most certain facts at the bottom and building more uncertain theories on laws that made up the groundwork of knowledge.

As doubts began to crack and shift the foundation of knowledge, some thinkers in the budding postmodern age decided that a completely objective perspective wasn't possible after all. In fact, everyone has bias to one degree or another, and this bias has an unavoidable effect on how we see the world.[9] In short, our culture could never guarantee that we had the whole truth, so postmodern thinkers stopped believing they would ever arrive at complete certainty. Instead, postmodernism taught that subjective individuals could learn from a variety of perspectives and continually test their conclusions in order to arrive at a better image of the truth, even if it's never completely clear.

In contemporary culture, this plays out in our need for a variety of news sources. The trusted evening news anchor[10] who delivers the facts has been challenged by a variety of voices online, on the radio, and on cable channels. Yet even with all these voices, we can't claim to possess the whole, even if we know more truth. For example, political conservatives accuse news outlets such as CNN of having a liberal bias, while liberals accuse Fox News Network of having a conservative bias. And then there's comedian Steven Colbert, who asserts that reality itself has a liberal bias. So in a postmodern world, we might conclude that no one believes in an independent and objective observer of facts anymore. Everyone has an angle, so from the postmodern standpoint, one authoritative source can't be considered reliable.

If postmodern thinkers reject the metaphor of knowledge as a solid foundation built on absolutely certain facts, what exactly should the new metaphor be? Many postmodern thinkers refer to knowledge as a web of beliefs.[11] This web more holistically represents various factors that influence what we know, yet it allows room to modify our beliefs when we find new truths and perspectives. Dan Stiver, a theologian with a foot in philosophy, says that the idea of a web of beliefs "allows for some beliefs to be more central and solid in relation to more peripheral beliefs."[12] In other words, this web offers a flexible way to arrange our beliefs, allowing room for them to change and shift over time. The beliefs in the center of the web depict the highest level of certainty and most important beliefs, while those on the outside are the most subject to being modified.

The idea of a web of beliefs helps us sort out doctrines of our Christian faith. We can focus on the most certain and most important while carefully evaluating new beliefs before incorporating them into our contextual theologies. For example, you might hear of the movement that focuses on God's desire to bring justice and mercy to the oppressed and poor (often called liberation theology), and add it to your web of beliefs. You might place this doctrine on the outer edge of your web, not moving it into the central position occupied by a more certain doctrine such as the Trinity. Still, liberation theology might gradually prompt you to conserve resources so you can share with people in need.

At the end of each chapter of this book, I've provided a web of contextual theology that places God and the Bible at the center, with Christian tradition and global Christians occupying points farther from the center. Culture remains on the fringes of contextual theology, offering insights into how we see the world but never replacing the more central parts.

As Christians in the postmodern context, we need to find ways to talk about and understand God. Yet many people outside of Christianity think that absolute truth is impossible to find, so they distrust Christians, perceiving us as biased by our faith. These challenges influence both how we think about God and how we share the gospel. Yet when postmodern thinkers deny the possibility of any real truth, any real conclusions about God, and any coherent way to explain our world, then Christians can answer by bringing the orienting story of God who reveals truth, who holds all things together, and who has overcome this world. As Christians, we can admit that our human knowledge of the truth is indeed limited. But we serve a God who has this world figured out, who knows the truth, the whole truth, and a whole lot more than the truth.

What We Can Say

Remember the common New Englander quip, It is what it is? We used this somewhat fatalistic phrase to help explain the modern era's view of language as a clear and precise representation of reality. Modern thinkers saw words for what they are—no more, no less. Through a modern lens, words had just one true interpretation, with no need for ambiguity or additional explanations.

In the postmodern world, language is viewed as a complex interaction of different meanings. People use words to convey meaning, but often a word can be used outside of its dictionary definition and applied in new ways. For example, have you ever said, "Just Google it"? What exactly does that mean? Of course, *Google* originally referred to a business made famous by its online search engine, but people eventually began using the business name as a verb to describe the act of using Google's search engine.

In the fictional story comparing Mayberry and *The Real World*, we caught a glimpse of how the meaning, understanding, and use of words can radically change a situation. Drew cited his backpacking days in Europe as one example of how trespassing could be defined differently than Andy and the people of Mayberry might define it. I based that part of the story on a real-life encounter a young German woman had while hiking through a field in Texas. Thinking that Americans were as relaxed as Germans about land use, she was surprised to find an angry man with a rifle demanding that she immediately remove herself from his property. We can see how language in the postmodern world doesn't usually carry a universal meaning but takes different forms depending on usage in a culture. Instead of a word being just what it is, the *use* of a word also helps determine its meaning, and that meaning can change over time as we use it.

For Christians, the postmodern perspective of language as a complex interaction of different meanings means that we need to constantly re-examine both our own language and biblical texts for unseen meanings or mischaracterizations. For example, Christians speak about faith as an act of believing. But one of my seminary professors suggested another nuance to the word often overlooked by Christians. In our course on the Pauline Epistles, he pointed out that the Greek word for "faith" can sometimes also be translated—when the context calls for it—as "faithfulness." So we can also say that a person has life through faithfulness (see Galatians 3:11), a concept that implies both the act of believing (see Galatians 3:2) and acts of continuing obedience.

When it comes to the complexity of language in the postmodern world, I also like the solution suggested by the philosophers Steven Best and Douglas Kellner, who say that we need to pursue the truth by reading and rereading, never claiming to have the definitive view, but humbly seeking the views of others to inform our own through critical evaluation.[13] Philosopher and noted author John Caputo adds that the best way to reach understanding is to continuously read and respond, never stopping to say we have it all figured out.[14]

Think about the ways we already take this approach. Even the fresh readings of familiar Scripture passages often give us new interpretations and insights. For example, every December pastors preach on a scant few verses about the birth of Christ, yet they regularly find new meanings, new angles, and new truths. This simple act of rereading and reinterpreting reveals the rich depths and complexities in language, especially the words of sacred Scripture.

So according to postmodernism we'll never quite have language figured out. The good news is that we can keep rereading and pressing on to find more of the truth. Still, we should keep in mind that saying we'll only understand part of what we hear or read isn't the same as saying that we're hearing or reading *nothing*. Such a surrender to relativism would give up too much to extreme postmodernism that wants to endlessly take our world apart, never settling on any particular truth because of the variety of possible meanings. As Christians doing contextual theology today, we need to remember that meaning truly does exist in the words of Scripture. We can rest in the truth we already possess while creating room for God's Spirit and the Christian community to give us new interpretations of Scripture too.

The Nature of Our World

In chapter 4, we noted that during the Middle Ages, people saw God at the center of the world's creation and function. The modern age replaced God with science, using laws, cycles, and theories to explain how the world ticks and why humanity exists. For modern thinkers, logic, science, and carefully constructed laws and procedures took God out of the picture.

While science remains a reliable guide for postmodern thinkers, the shift from orderly laws and proof through the scientific method to the probability of quantum mechanics has caused some philosophers to wonder if our world contains a good dose of relativity, chaos, and mystery (although some committed scientists disagree[15]). And even if we think we understand who we are and why we're here, many cultures and people groups with different stories challenge the dominance of our stories. This became apparent after the collapse of colonial power in the mid-1900s uncovered a wide array of beliefs and perspectives that challenged the worldviews of the West. These shifts in science and history tell philosophers that one story doesn't fit all, and perhaps our world isn't so easy to explain.

A look at U.S. history demonstrates the difficulty of understanding our world through one all-inclusive story. While scholars in the modern age worked extremely hard to be objective, they naturally presented conclusions from their research that matched their own culture and beliefs. Past American historians, for example, presented the westward movement of European immigrants and Americans from the east as expansion. While technically accurate and not necessarily wrong, the word *expansion* doesn't tell the whole story and ignores the perspective of Native American and Hispanic residents of these lands, who would more likely characterize these settlers as invaders. And while American settlers were guided by the story of their destiny to settle the land from sea to shining sea, the story Native Americans might tell would be very different. They became the victims of broken treaties, massacres, and confinement to reservations. If "objective" observers couldn't represent all of the perspectives and stories in America's history, we need to question whether any attempt at characterizing the nature of our world can avoid gaps and oversights. We can arrive at part of the picture, but some unknowns will always exist.

Postmodern thinkers who observe the revisions made to historical narratives of the modern age conclude that our times have changed. The stories of other cultures provide hints that our world is a rather random, disconnected, and even chaotic collection of narratives.[16] This doesn't imply that supposedly objective disciplines such as science or history aren't valid. Rather, postmodern philosophers simply believe that we need more than one reasonable perspective to explain our world. The nature of our world today often leaves room for options beyond the one story of modernism. And it might even include a gap for a God who not only created the world but also remains very involved in it.

Gaps in knowledge make up a part of the postmodern changes in our world today. But the conclusions that researchers, scientists, and scholars come to aren't the only elements called into question in the postmodern age. Theologian and philosopher Trevor Hart believes that even the methods used to arrive at scientific or historical conclusions—though often reliable—will generally fail to deliver the kind of certainty thought possible in the modern age. Postmodern philosophers like Hart believe that seekers of knowledge can't objectively observe data but instead run their thinking through their own belief systems and sometimes inadvertently influence their results.[17] Simply put, our world consists of much more than what we can test and explain through logic, research, or science.

With the questions postmodernism brings about our understanding of the world, Christians have an opportunity to explain the nature of our world by filling in some of the unexplained gaps and mysteries with God. Instead of pitting the Christian faith against science, history, or any other discipline, we have an opportunity to learn from those fields, recognizing that arriving at the truth requires help from multiple perspectives.

Of course, when we consider multiple perspectives, we run the risk of adopting a fragmented view of the world where only random puzzle pieces exist and there's no real way to put them together. While Christians can certainly acknowledge the complexity in creation, we can't follow postmodern thinkers who believe our world consists of unordered chaos without true meaning, purpose, or design. So we face the challenge of explaining our world with some humility while also believing that God has put together something meaningful and orderly—even if we'll never quite figure it out.

LIVING IN A POSTMODERN WORLD

Now that we have a handle on the basic elements of postmodernism and its effect on our world, we'll look in greater detail at how the church has fared in the move from modern to postmodern. As Christians who seek to faithfully study God—to form theology—we must try to understand our world and the effect of the world on our faith. This permits us to uncover blind spots, biases, and any other variables that meddle with the way we approach God, read the Bible, or interact with other Christians.

Once we understand where we come from and who we are, we can then step into the important task of knowing God through Christian theology.

▶ ▶ ▶ FOR FURTHER READING

- *A Primer on Postmodernism* (Grand Rapids, MI: Eerdmans, 1996), by Stanley Grenz
- *Mapping Postmodernism: A Survey of Christian Options* (Downers Grove, IL: InterVarsity, 2003), by Robert Greer
- *The Cambridge Companion to Postmodernism* (Cambridge, England: Cambridge University Press, 2004), by Steven Connor

For additional resources and discussion, see http://inamirrordimly .com/coffeehouse-theology/chapter-5.

A Web of Theology

This web illustrates the interconnected nature of Christian theology's sources and contexts.

Current chapter topic will be in bold.

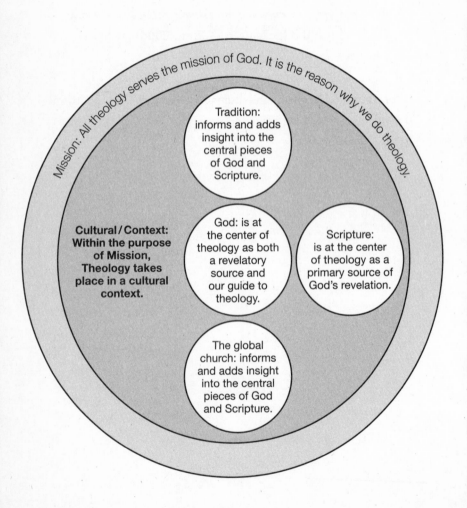

Mission: All theology serves the mission of God. It is the reason why we do theology.

Tradition: informs and adds insight into the central pieces of God and Scripture.

Cultural/Context: Within the purpose of Mission, Theology takes place in a cultural context.

God: is at the center of theology as both a revelatory source and our guide to theology.

Scripture: is at the center of theology as a primary source of God's revelation.

The global church: informs and adds insight into the central pieces of God and Scripture.

THEOLOGY AND CULTURE

Moving from Who We Are to Who God Is

"I think the main questions we should ask are What is sin? Who is Jesus? and How do you get to heaven?" declared Cindy.

My classmate David and I sat on the other side of the booth from Cindy, and almost in unison, the two of us shifted uneasily. The three of us were planning an evangelism event for a seminary class on — what else — evangelism. Our assignment: Put together an event where you can clearly present the gospel and then report back to the class on what happened.

We didn't feel comfortable pulling off a bait-and-switch event that promises one thing and then drops in the gospel, like the Super Bowl outreach that involves slipping in a brief evangelism DVD during half time for the benefit of your heathen friends. So we decided that we'd conduct a survey to get a discussion going. Besides, we really did care what people thought about God. If they expressed interest, they could stick around after the survey to hear more.

Cindy wanted to cut to the chase—convicting our unsuspecting subjects of their sin, pointing them to Jesus, and then closing the deal all in one holy swoop. Of course, many people have done this before and insist it's the way to go. But David and I didn't think this would work in our town. After taking a few classes on theology and culture, we realized that controlling a conversation, focusing on just the facts of Christianity, and ignoring the perspectives of our audience wouldn't fly in our culture. While all three of us wanted to arrive at the place where people trust in Jesus, we needed to find a way to make Jesus accessible for our postmodern audience filled with skeptics. They'd bristle at an aggressive presentation of Christian truth that ignored their thoughts on the subject. In short, we persuaded Cindy that we needed to write up a different kind of survey.

Our little attempt actually worked quite well. We came up with a short survey of just eight questions. We focused on the beliefs of our audience, asking what they think of God, how they connect with God, and what keeps them away from God. We ended by asking if they were satisfied with where they were or if they wanted to know more about God. With this question, we entered into some great conversations with people around town. Cindy ended up with a crowd of high school students gathered around her at a local café, all sharing what they thought and politely listening to her talk about God. I had a conversation with one person whose Christian relatives seemed mean and judgmental and another who really wanted to know what I believe about Jesus. In both cases, I presented a faithful picture of Jesus by sharing my own experiences with God and the truth of Scripture.

We knew our effort touched some nerves when a minivan screeched to a halt next to us, the door swung open, and a high school–aged boy screamed, "There is no God!" Even if we didn't end up with a stream of converts parading behind us down the street, we succeeded in showing roughly thirty people that Christians will listen to them and answer their questions and concerns about God. In a few cases, some more inquisitive people learned about the gospel and had a chance to hear our stories of living by faith. With the exception of the minivan crew, the people we talked to never seemed irritated by our questions and often shared openly what they believed. Many asked us for our take on Jesus. This attempt to listen to people's experiences and doubts provides just one example of how a contextual approach to theology can make the Christian message relevant in our world today.

Let's look briefly at how culture influences our faith and how Christianity functioned in the modern age, during the transition to the postmodern age, and now during culture's complete shift to the postmodern era. Then we'll look at three ways Christians can respond to postmodernism, landing on the best approach for doing contextual theology in the postmodern age.

THE INFLUENCE OF CULTURE ON CHRISTIANITY

Just as I learned to rethink evangelism because of the culture in my town, we can see how our changing culture brings shifts to theology. For example, look at the changes in the way recent films portray Jesus: the holy hippie Jesus in *Godspell*, the hapless fool Jesus in *Jesus Christ Superstar*, and the "authentic" Jesus who speaks Aramaic in *The Passion of the Christ*. *Godspell* embodies the enthusiasm of the Jesus movement in the 1970s, while *Jesus Christ Superstar* reflects the views of liberal scholars—products of the modern age's reliance on science alone—who reimagined Jesus without his supernatural qualities. *The Passion of the Christ* reflects the ideas of conservative Christian scholars of the late twentieth century who worked hard to recreate the exact historical setting of Scripture. Each reveals certain features of a context, hinting that culture quite naturally seeps into theology—even the theology of playwrights and movie producers.

Christians aren't immune from this seeping cultural influence either. Over time, we can easily overlook the shifts and changes of our views of Jesus and how we practice our faith. Culture sometimes changes us before we realize it.

The evolving nature of Christianity shouldn't surprise us. We can't hope to keep the church precisely like its early predecessors any more than we can keep bellbottoms or togas in style. To a certain degree, we can feel some relief in knowing that the church changes over time, because not all change is bad. In spite of the worship wars of the 1990s, most people realize that we can use rock music in church today just as the nineteenth-century church used the piano and present-day Africans use drums for worship.

During the modern age, when culture placed a high priority on reason and the scientific method, the church naturally tagged along and adopted the best the world had to offer. This posed no problem as long as Christians didn't compromise the call of Christ with these new ways of thinking. Still, we hit a problem if we begin to connect elements of culture to Christianity without criticism or evaluation. Now that we've explored the shift from modernism to post-modernism, we can begin the process of re-evaluating our theology. This allows us to make sure that holdover modern influences aren't masquerading as part of Christianity. We can also be sure that our message remains relevant but not compromised by today's culture.

CHRISTIANITY IN AN AGE OF REASON

One example of the modern age's infiltrating Christianity was the practice of relying on the objectivity of just one observer, someone who studies Scripture and figures out a meaning or interpretation without necessarily paying attention to interpretations from the past or elsewhere in the world.[1] This practice began to take shape during the Protestant Reformation and took root as the modern age progressed. It pitted individual interpretations of Scripture against the views of the official church in Rome.

Reliance primarily on the reasoning powers of individuals to figure out the Bible generally prevailed in the Protestant branch of Christianity into the 1900s and still continues in many quarters. While I have no objections to reason or individual Bible study (I'm putting both into practice throughout this book), the modern age tempted Christians to rely largely on their own reasoning not only in understanding the Bible but also in deciding how to apply it. What's more, when individuals in the modern age studied the Bible, they often read it like a contemporary history or work of literature, instead of reading it as ancient literature. This sometimes led to overly literal readings of books such as Isaiah and Revelation that likely speak of spiritual events but that some interpret as predicting literal events in the future.[2]

In addition, some Christians expressed skepticism about spiritual gifts and miracles. While we can attribute some of this cynicism to frauds who used the gospel to make a buck, much grows out of the modern doubt that God intervenes directly with our world. As the modern age removed the mystery and spirituality of the Middle Ages, many Christians went so far as teaching that miracles and other manifestations of the Spirit no longer happen in the world. Some liberal Christians even claimed that miracles in the Bible didn't happen at all, relying on science to explain or discredit the events.

The modern age placed pressure on Christians to meet the world on its own terms and even attempted to demand evidence or a reasonable basis for believing in Jesus. While Christians in the later 1900s began to present their own stories to share the gospel as part of a shift to the postmodern age, popular books in support of Christianity such as *The New Evidence That Demands a Verdict: Christianity Beyond a Reasonable Doubt* (Nashville: Thomas Nelson, 1999) and *The Case for Christ* (Grand Rapids, MI: Zondervan, 1998) show the remaining marks of the modern age's reliance on reason and even scientific proofs.

In fact, many of us still want to prove that our faith has reason and evidence behind it. While reason and evidence serve as useful tools, sometimes we give them too much weight, when instead we should add tools such as additional perspectives from Christian tradition and believers around the world, as well as the guidance of the Holy Spirit.

We can use the terms of today's culture and work within its boundaries as long as this two-way dialogue helps us understand God and spread the gospel in both relevant and prophetic ways. If we learn anything by looking at Christians in the modern age, we can see that culture influences our theology, so we must remain vigilant and thoughtful.

TENSION IN A CHANGING WORLD

As Christians in the modern world grew increasingly dependent on individual reason, they experienced many positive changes, including the distribution of the Bible in the common language of the people for personal study. During the Protestant Reformation, Christians began to deny church authorities their power because the populace could read the Bible and make up their own minds. On the upside, everyone could study God and learn about him. However, on the downside, modernity also brought rampant individualism and theological elitism among different groups, fragmenting Christians and even leading to the persecution and murder of believers from different denominations. Remember, for example, that settlers came to America from Europe in search of religious freedom.

One of the lasting marks of modernity on the theology of the church is the conservative-liberal theological split during the early 1900s. According to Christian philosophy professor Nancey Murphy, modernism forced "theologians to choose Scripture or experience as the source of this special, foundational class of beliefs. Conservatives have chosen Scripture; liberals, characteristically, have chosen experience."[3] During this time, theological liberals tossed the historicity of the Bible to the wind, opened the door to all manner of interpretations, embraced a social agenda aimed at helping the poor, and focused on experiencing God.

When theological conservatives caught wind of the liberal abandonment of the Bible, they responded by embracing Scripture and an extreme reliance on the inerrancy of the biblical text as the very foundation of Christianity. Prior to this point in church history, inerrancy rarely became a point of contention. Christians simply trusted the Bible, assuming that on the whole Scripture arrived at an accurate account of events and teachings. However, after Christians embraced the modern agenda and tried to prove the foundation for their faith, they began to scrutinize the Bible to make sure every detail lined up perfectly. Christians began to worry about the exact chronology of the events listed in the four Gospels (especially the events of Jesus' last days), the precise numbers listed in Scripture, the chronologies of Israel's and Judah's kings, and any other hint that the Bible might contain the smallest error. In other words, we began to read the Bible like a scientific text.[4]

The conservative and liberal factions of Christianity continued to fracture and divide during the twentieth century, leading to denominations and subgroups within denominations. For example, some liberal churches embraced conservative theology or at least arrived at a middle ground known as neo-orthodoxy. On the other hand, fundamentalist groups emerged among conservative churches, separating themselves from any hint of the "world" in order to remain pure.

To this day, the church hasn't figured out how to reconcile individualism and unity. Why do we have so many disagreements, divisions, and books outlining the various views on baptism, the end times, women in ministry, homosexuality, and even the orthodoxy of the Orthodox Church? Perhaps expecting to arrive at a clear and simple meaning from the Bible creates an impossible situation that simply leads to more divisions. We might say that the modern world gave us the wonderful gift of the Bible in the hands of the masses, yet it also showed us that individuals aren't quite capable of handling it on their own.

CHRISTIANS IN POSTMODERN CULTURE

So what do we do with our faith in the age of postmodernism? Some Christians think that postmodern culture provides the answers to Christianity's woes. Other Christians view postmodern culture as a threat that they must oppose at any cost. In a sense, both groups are wrong.

Remember, we're interested in contextual theology: understanding God within a particular context. Postmodernism influences our cultural context, and we need to figure out a way to deal with it. The postmodern era can be both friend and foe — just like the modern age, which put the Bible into the hands of the average person but also caused Christians to stop relying on God's supernatural intervention in our world.

So as we try to figure out the best way to understand God and to spread his truth in a postmodern world — in other words, as we practice contextual theology — we have a lot at stake. We face some dangers, and we can enjoy some benefits. For starters, we can correct some of the syncretism between the modern age and Christianity. Rather than thinking of Bible study only as a private matter done alone, Christians need to study Scripture in community with other Christians. In addition, we need to examine our history and traditions, listen to believers from other cultures, and open ourselves to the Holy Spirit's leading. We must reckon with the complexity of our world and our theology, recognizing that we possess more truth when we include voices other than our own. Theology in our post-modern times also requires reading and rereading Scripture so we can always sharpen and correct our interpretations.

On the other hand, contextual theologians—and remember, that's all of us—will face new problems in the postmodern age. If we take in and value too many perspectives at once and never work toward arriving at some kind of belief or doctrine, we'll easily fall into a kind of relativism that might boast tolerance but runs short on actual truth. And if we run short on truth—actual beliefs we can rest in—we run the risk of never putting much of anything into practice.

In addition, the practice of rereading and reinterpreting Scripture and listening to a diversity of voices can also backfire into accepting doctrines from outside the Christian fold.[5] As contextual theologians, we also run the risk of separating from other Christians who accuse us of using a worldly approach to Scripture, while we subconsciously view them as less relevant or enlightened in matters of Christianity and culture. Of course, the problem of division cuts both ways.

THREE RESPONSES TO POSTMODERNISM[6]

When I think back to the street evangelism survey project from my seminary days, I'm reminded of three ways Christians typically relate to postmodernism: separation, awareness, and dialogue. The first chooses to remain unaware of the influences of culture or simply chooses to separate from it. The second learns about cultural influences and might change a few ways of thinking or acting, but does not get into contextual theology for the most part. And the third tries to learn from culture while speaking God's truth into it. I want to point out that in all three categories there are committed followers of Jesus who accomplish tremendous work for God.

Although I want to stress that we'll find people who truly love Jesus within all three of these approaches, I believe that dialoguing with culture presents the best possibilities for practicing contextual theology. I want to be a good postmodern thinker and state right up front that I'm personally partial to the dialogue approach. Many Christians are trying to figure out theology and context, and it's hard to settle on black-and-white boundaries to determine whether or not we've succeeded. If I can offer one caution, contextual theologians should be wary of abandoning the central doctrines of the faith passed on to us—if we take our Christian traditions seriously, hopefully we won't fall into that trap.

Let's briefly look at each of these ways that we can relate our faith to the postmodern age.

Separating from Culture

Christians who claim to be separated from culture[7] face the danger of not noticing its influence on their thinking. In fact, theologian and minister Craig Van Gelder points out that no culturally pure expression of Christianity exists.[8] In other words, no matter how much we ignore culture, culture doesn't ignore us. We can't help but absorb some of the thinking and values of our times. And not paying attention to these influences means misguided theologians can sometimes spread a theology they believe is culturally pure when it's not.

In fact, when I talk to Christians who express fears about contextual theology in postmodern times, many of their reservations stem from unnoticed influences of the modern age on their thinking.

While Christians who separate themselves from culture won't ruin the good doctrines passed on to them, they do run the risk of not reevaluating some of the more questionable doctrines they inherit. In the postmodern age, these Christians end up poorly equipped to share the gospel in a relevant manner.

Awareness of Culture

Some Christians become very aware of culture, wanting to be a light to the world by sharing the gospel in relevant ways.[9] These Christians generally leave their theology intact, and focus more on applying and sharing their beliefs in ways that are culturally relevant. In other words, they spend little time considering how culture forms a lens that we understand God through, and instead view culture as a tool to share the gospel and to shape how they gather and worship. They generally don't change the content of their theology, so they miss out on opportunities to correct the mistakes of past theologians and leave themselves vulnerable to the unknown influences of today's culture that can eventually seep into their beliefs.

While we most likely won't see any new heresies come from this group, they'll struggle down the road as their lack of attention to the influence of culture on theology catches up with them.

Dialoguing with Culture

In my own evangelical circles, I've noticed that the favorite way to definitively settle a theological debate involves assembling a collection of theological heavyweights and assigning each a chapter to write. They then collectively settle the matter at hand.

I have a problem with this approach. If you read enough of the resulting books, the same names start to show up a lot. When I look at the names and credentials of these authors, I notice a few things that make me nervous as a contextual theologian: Most are white, male, American, and theological conservatives. Does anyone else see that excluding African Americans, women, Latin Americans, and people from other theological camps makes for a lopsided discussion?[10] While these theologians have a lot to teach us—more than I could ever whip up—I feel a little short-changed.

Christians need more than a panel of homogenous experts. We need a robust conversation with our culture and Christians from a variety of backgrounds, denominations, countries, and even times in history. Why do I think this? Because I think the best way to relate Christian faith with the postmodern age is to dialogue with culture.

As Christians, when we discourse with culture, we not only recognize the values of our times, but we also can confront the more troublesome values with our theology. We realize that culture serves as a lens that we look through both to see the world and to see and relate to God. When we dialogue with culture, we gain an understanding of culture that enables us either to learn from it and make our theology relevant or to challenge the parts of culture that oppose the teachings of Scripture.

In other words, as we interact with the values of postmodern culture, we naturally become wary of basing our beliefs on the views of theologians from one country, gender, race, age group, and background. A healthy dialogue with postmodernism helps us become aware of the ignored voices of the church, especially minorities both from today and from our history. And keep in mind that broadening the conversation doesn't imply that we reject past doctrines or theologians, just that we add to or refine them: We value those contributions, but we look for more as well.

Dialoguing with culture changes how we think about God, but it also changes our practice. My seminary group's evangelism project provides an example of engaging postmodern culture in a way that changed our approach to presenting the gospel. We created room for conversation and a diversity of opinions and allowed our audience to have the first say. Still, when it came time to clearly state the truth of Christianity, we didn't fall back, because a point comes when we must take up the prophetic calling of speaking God's truth in our culture.

Of course, the dialogue approach to Christian theology in the postmodern age has both advantages and disadvantages. On the plus side, we learn that we don't have the final word on theology, we have a lot to learn from others, and we need to keep rereading the Bible in light of these findings. However, sometimes we simply need to be the unpopular ones who inform skeptics that the Bible in fact is true, God does have moral standards, and that Jesus came to earth to save us and plans on returning some day, so we best take him seriously. While people in a postmodern culture don't exactly want to hear these truths, they need to.

Contextual theology might help us see new aspects of God and his plan of redemption. But in the end, it still boils down to whether or not we'll follow him and live as ambassadors for Christ here on earth, no matter what the culture might be.[11]

FROM WHO WE ARE TO WHO GOD IS

Let's review the first steps we've taken as contextual theologians.

We understand our context—who we are and how we think.

We know the modern age that shaped much of our world is being replaced by a way of thinking often labeled postmodernism.

We know that postmodernism values a diversity of perspectives, countering the modern tendency to seek an objective and universal view of the world.

We see the value of studying and reinterpreting Scripture while in conversation with other Christians and our traditions, even if we stay cautious about departing from the essential doctrines of our faith.

We recognize that seeking one objective perspective of the world can silence minority voices and generally blind us to a world of possibilities.

We keep in mind that more truth exists and can be found, even if we can't comprehend all of it from our limited perspective.

And looming over all of these discussions about theology and culture is God—our God who calls us to follow in a particular time and place, the God we seek to understand after we know who we are and how we see the world. In fact, if we want to form and practice contextual theology, then we need to move more deeply into the sources of theology. And we begin with God.

As Christians, we have an opportunity to know God. Even better, God gives us opportunities to share him with others. And if I can top that, we actually have the Holy Spirit dwelling within us, enabling us to complete the work of Jesus on earth. Jesus said, "I tell you the truth, anyone who has faith in me will do what I have been doing. He will do even greater things than these, because I am going to the Father" (John 14:12, see also 14:15-19).

That's a pretty staggering promise! But we need to realize that it represents Jesus' vision for us, his followers.

Jesus makes it abundantly clear that any success we have in completing his mission on earth rests on his influence in us through the Holy Spirit. As we do contextual theology in order to understand God and to share his message with others, we must keep in mind that God empowers us to do his work.

In fact, all of our faith as Christians rests on the work of God:

sending the Holy Spirit, sending prophets, inspiring the writers of the Bible, and making repentance and new life possible. At every turn, we come face to face with God. Even as we delve into contextual theology in postmodern times, we can't help but come to grips with the reality of our God who knows all truth, sees all things, and has complete understanding.

We must begin with God because God not only answers the questions of our times, but because he hovers over all that we are as Christians. Without God's first step toward us, we stand helpless in any quest to understand our Creator and Savior.

▶ ▶ ▶ FOR FURTHER READING

- *Beyond Foundationalism: Shaping Theology in a Postmodern Context* (Louisville, KY: Westminster, 2007), by Stanley Grenz and John Franke
- *Renewing the Center: Evangelical Theology in a Post-Theological Era* (Grand Rapids, MI: Baker, 2006), by Stanley Grenz
- *Above All Earthly Pow'rs: Christ in a Postmodern World* (Grand Rapids, MI: Eerdmans, 2006), by David Wells
- *Ancient-Future Faith: Rethinking Evangelicalism for a Postmodern World* (Grand Rapids, MI: Baker, 1999), by Robert Webber
- *The Gospel in a Pluralist Society* (Grand Rapids, MI: Eerdmans, 1989), by Lesslie Newbigin
- *The Cambridge Companion to Postmodern Theology* (New York: Cambridge University Press, 2003), edited by Kevin J. Vanhoozer
- *The Next Reformation: Why Evangelicals Must Embrace Postmodernity* (Grand Rapids, MI: Baker: 2004), by Carl Raschke

- *Who's Afraid of Postmodernism? Taking Derrida, Lyotard, and Foucault to Church* (Grand Rapids, MI: Baker, 2006), by James K.A. Smith

For additional resources and discussion, see http://inamirror-dimly.com/coffeehouse-theology/chapter-6.

Chapter 7

CONTEXTUAL THEOLOGY WITH GOD AT THE CENTER

When I was in college, I became friends with Kevin. While Kevin expressed an interest in God, he said he didn't really know how a relationship with God worked. He once told me, "Even though I grew up in church, it seemed like religion and rules and traditions. I don't feel like I really know God. To be honest, I don't sense that God really knows me."

As a member of a crowd that hung out together, Kevin joined us one evening for a time of worship songs, one of our group's regular practices.

I don't remember anything unique happening that night. Like Christian college students all over the country have done thousands of times, we just prayed and worshipped with the songs we knew. Still, after that evening I had a chance to catch up with Kevin, and he shared with me, "That night of singing worship songs was the first time I really experienced God." After that he began to pray and to seek God actively.

Kevin's story points to the very first step—and the constant focus, for that matter—in doing theology: knowing God. Christians believe that God searches for people who will follow (see Luke 19:10) and obey (John 10:10-15), and I believe that's exactly what happened to Kevin. God reached out through worship, Kevin responded, and he then sought a relationship with God.

Enter theology.

For Christians, theology is the way we respond to God's revealing himself to us. While the primary source of God's revelation is Scripture, he also reveals himself to us through tradition and the insights of global Christians. In other words, God uses all three sources of information to reveal himself, but the Bible serves as the most important piece of revelation.[1]

Before we open the Bible, Christian theology requires a first step of faith, a conversion to God, and an indwelling of the Holy Spirit. The Holy Spirit opens us to the truth of Scripture and to the ways of God (see Philippians 3:15; 1 Corinthians 2:6-16). In fact, if we set out to understand God, what better guide can we have than the very Spirit of God, who reveals the deep truths of God as we step into theology? God reveals his truth to us as we listen to the Spirit and read Scripture.

Maybe I'm making this too complicated. Most simply put, *we understand God through a relationship with God.* We place God at the center of contextual theology in the postmodern age—in any age for that matter—because God possesses knowledge of truth and reveals it to us, although it often comes in bits and pieces. Postmodernism reminds us that we don't have complete access to the truth. But as Christians, we know that God does.

GOD: THE ONE WHO REVEALS TRUTH

You know God is up to something when one verse of Scripture completely changes your life. For most of my Christian walk, I didn't give much thought to how God uses Scripture as a way to reveal himself. Or how the Holy Spirit can take a few words and then slice them into people's lives, changing their relationship with the Lord forever (see Hebrews 4:12).

But one night when I was nineteen, the Spirit of God hit me. I sometimes call this my Martin Luther moment. I recall reading the book of Romans, the same book that sparked the famous Reformer's theological revolution. Sitting on my floor, I found myself reading Romans 3:21 over and over again: "But now a righteousness from God, apart from law, has been made known, to which the Law and the Prophets testify."

At this time, I was light-years away from an inkling about the point of this biblical book. Most likely I completely misunderstood the references to the Law, and I probably could only name two prophets . . . tops. Yet I sensed something important was taking place, so I meditated on the passage—not even knowing that I was actually meditating.

The words "righteousness from God" stuck in my mind. I couldn't shake them. They happily camped out in my head, challenging my notion of Christianity and reminding me over and over again that I'd approached this following Jesus business all wrong.

I took a walk. I wept. I laughed. I sang. My connection to God finally made sense. Righteousness from God! God revealed to me that this was the good news of his gospel. Interestingly, the key word was *from*, rather than *righteousness* or *God*. *From* made me realize that we must completely depend on God for righteousness. We don't have to earn God's favor. Instead, God wants us to live by faith in the righteousness that only our Savior can provide.

I don't know how I figured this out. But of course, I didn't. God did! Through prayerful meditation, I learned my first lesson in theology: that God speaks to us through Scripture. He reveals truth and guides our understanding.

This role of God tells us something about truth as we do theology in the postmodern context: Even if we don't have access to all of the truth, God does. And he reveals truth to those who seek it.[2]

As we look at our faith in a postmodern context, we need to be willing to examine our definition of truth. Or more accurately, we need to re-examine our source of truth. While the Bible serves as one of our main sources of truth about God, we need to keep in mind that as the Bible was written through divine inspiration, we need to depend on God to show us truth when we read and interpret his Word. While we look to Scripture to reveal God, God actually reveals Scripture to us. In addition, God not only knows the truth, he also *is* the truth—something I still can't quite wrap my brain around. Or to express this another way: To say that God is the only absolute or certain truth in the world means that absolute truth does exist in God, but we don't have complete access to the truth. God alone possesses absolute truth and only reveals portions of it to us (see 1 Corinthians 13:12).

When we read the Old Testament, we can clearly and unmistakably distinguish between the roles of God and man. Whether in the form of a flaming pot, burning bush, powerful soldier, or gentle wind, God takes the initiative. God serves as the revealer, the one who opens our eyes to the truth, the one who gives Scripture value, meaning, and application. Jesus pointed out our need to rely on God's Spirit: "But when he, the Spirit of truth, comes, he will guide you into all truth. He will not speak on his own; he will speak only what he hears, and he will tell you what is yet to come" (John 16:13).

When Jesus stated "I am the way, the truth, and the life" (John 14:6), he provided an opportunity to explain God in our postmodern context in both a relevant and prophetic way. In terms of relevance, "I am the truth" affirms that we have a limited perspective of truth. In fact, his statement rescues us from claiming to have an objective view about truth. However, we maintain a prophetic voice in our culture by asserting that we know real, objective truth exists, and that truth can be found in Jesus.

We'll simply never be able to attain the absolutely transcendent view of the world that God possesses, and I believe Christians can agree with this. Even with the Bible in hand, we must admit that we don't have the ability to know truth from a completely objective and certain perspective. As Christians, this should humble but not discourage us. Admitting that we don't have total access to objective truth isn't the same as affirming relativism. Instead, it just means that our knowledge is a more limited, local truth. Theologian and philosopher Merold Westphal provides some valuable guidance along these lines: "Truth" as a principle or law apart from God *might* not be accessible to us, but surely truth does exist, and so we press forward with the pursuit of truth. Westphal said that while we can never preside over truth (absolute and objective truth, that is) or grasp it in a complete way, we should never abandon the pursuit of truth or deny its existence altogether.[3]

Anyone who denies the existence of truth stands on shaky ground. When postmodernism takes us to that extreme, as Christians, we can't follow along. Yet Christians can agree with postmodern thinkers in saying that finite humans simply can't ascend to the heights where we can know absolute truth.

As we study the Bible, learn from other Christians, and form theology in the postmodern context, we face limitations in understanding truth, understanding language, and even explaining the nature of our world. Rather than denying the existence of truth or an explanation for the nature of our world, we can look to God as the keeper of all knowledge and truth. In fact, this keeps us humble in our pursuit of theology, because we know our theology can never quite be complete, and will always need corrections. We can continue to pursue theology, prayerfully studying the Bible and running our interpretations past Christian traditions and global theology in order to test our findings. Sometimes, we might change our beliefs, while at other times we'll validate the soundness of the beliefs we already hold.

Through it all though, we must keep God at the center because we know that God has ultimate access to the truth and reveals it to us. By keeping God at the center of theology, we rely on the Holy Spirit to reveal the truth and apply it to our lives. The Spirit helps us to reflect on God's truth but also to reflect or imitate God as we live under his influence.

Of course we can't always expect that we'll just happen to stumble into the Holy Spirit as I did while reading Romans that night. We can't separate prayer from Bible study. As we entrust our theology and our lives to God, we can see that prayer changes who we are, how we read Scripture, and how we apply the revealed truth from Scripture to our lives. In short, Christian theology runs dry without prayer.

KEEPING GOD AT THE CENTER THROUGH PRAYER AND MEDITATION

Perhaps one of the most horrendous, humbling, and exhausting things we all do every now and then, moving reminds us that we're materialistic packrats who probably need to have an unsupervised yard sale in our homes. During a miserably wet spring in Vermont, where the earth seemed to be repelling the sweeping showers constantly pelting the landscape, Julie and I were set to move out of our rental house into the home we purchased.

We closed the deal just in time to move before we had to be out of our rental property. I found a reliable local rental truck company — having learned my lesson during our last move about using a certain national chain — and set the pickup date for the truck. Our house looked like a haven for prohibition smugglers, with our vast library stacked in liquor boxes and shreds of cardboard littering the floor as a result of our rabbits' ripping the boxes to shreds. We were ready to move but lacked a moving crew.

As I prayed about the situation one morning, the Lord brought to mind some friends of our family who lived about three hours away. I asked God if he could send them our way, yet, because of the long drive, I didn't feel like we should directly ask them to help us move. The Wednesday before our scheduled move, one of the men called. "Hey, Ed," he said, "I was just praying, and I sensed the Lord telling me to come help you guys move." A wave of relief rushed over me. God had heard my prayer and moved — literally. As if a friend from three hours away wasn't enough, another couple offered to help us. All in all, God worked a miracle. During uncertain times, he revealed himself through prayer and managed to even toss in a few surprises on moving day.

After God answered that simple prayer, I began to notice other prayers in Scripture. These were wild and outlandish prayers, such as prayers for deliverance from foreign invaders, the superpowers of their time. Not only did God hear these prayers, he followed through and brought clear answers. In the case of King Hezekiah (see Isaiah 36–37), God also brought deliverance. As I continued to grow in my relationship with the Lord through prayer, my study of Scripture changed as well, as if God wanted to give me one more nudge to seek the Holy Spirit in my reading of Scripture.

Through our prayers, God reveals himself to us in both large and small ways. That's why prayer is essential as we approach theology.

We can think of it this way: Theology without prayer is like trying to drive without gas or a destination. God provides both the fuel and the purpose for theology. Without a thriving relationship with God, Bible study will be empty. So from start to finish, we need to surround theology with prayer and meditation.

Without God's driving our pursuit of him, less noble motives can enter the void and lead to an abuse of Scripture and possibly of ourselves and other Christians. Besides carving out time to pray or meditate, Christians can actively integrate prayer into their study of Scripture in some very specific ways. For example, we can prayerfully meditate on Scripture using lectio divina and the monastic Liturgy of the Hours made popular for lay readers as *The Divine Hours*.

Lectio divina, an ancient practice of spiritual reading, enables Christians to pray right from the Bible. Many Christians have redis-covered this method, which requires only a Bible. I like how lectio divina effectively creates room for the Holy Spirit to speak through the selected passage.[4] Father Thomas Keating, a speaker and author on contemplative prayer, describes this practice:

> A passage is read out loud three or four times followed by
> two or three minutes of silence. After each reading the
> participants apply themselves inwardly to the text in speci-
> fied ways. After the first reading, they become aware of
> a word or phrase. After the second they reflect about the
> meaning or significance of the text. After the third reading,
> they respond in spontaneous prayer. After the fourth read-
> ing, they simply rest in God's presence.[5]

Jeanne Guyon, a noted Christian mystic, advocates a similar use of Scripture for prayer so that the believer can experience Christ deep within.[6] Guyon advises readers to read through a small portion of

Scripture very slowly, then notes, "You do not move from one passage to another, not until you have sensed the very heart of what you have read. You may then want to take that portion of Scripture that has touched you and turn it into prayer."[7]

If these practices sound a little intimidating, for a few bucks you can pick up *The Message//REMIX: Solo: An Uncommon Devotional*, which arranges this contemporary Scripture translation into readings based on lectio divina to walk you through the practice of praying Scripture.

Personally, I'm particularly fond of *The Divine Hours* series of prayer books compiled by Phyllis Tickle. Tickle abridges the lengthy Liturgy of the Hours practiced by monastic orders into a collection of prayers and Scripture readings. She includes prayers from Christians throughout history and around the world, a real plus in contextual theology. Readings take place in the morning, afternoon, and evening, as well as a brief reading before retiring for the night called the compline. Tickle keeps the readings relatively short, making it easy to meditate on psalms, gospel readings, and other small parts of the Bible. This prayer manual, available in three volumes, is also published online at www.explorefaith.org/prayer/fixed/.[8] I find these relatively short readings a helpful way to start my day with Scripture and also to meditate on Scripture and to spark prayer throughout my day as I pray through the various offices. Uniting Scripture with prayer keeps us connected to God, the one at the center of our theology, who reveals truth.

From the Center to Scripture

Christians in the postmodern world reject relativism by believing that God stands as the absolute — the one who knows all timeless truth. When we begin with God as the center of theology, we make a statement: God is the giver of life and truth.

What's more, we rely on the revelation of the Holy Spirit to open our eyes to God and to then lead us into the truth. As we study the Bible and interact with other views from history and around the world, we can remember that we aren't simply concerned with being "right" and nailing down the truth. We're in a relationship with God, so we press on with theology in order to know God. God reveals the truth to us, and so we seek him, keeping focused on our Savior and Creator as the center of everything.

The key to seeking God's truth is a vibrant prayer life that ranges from quiet moments of prayerful Scripture reading to Spirit-led meditation on large portions of the Bible to listening for the voice of God as we wait patiently. When reading God's revealed Scripture, we seek to link with the revealing Spirit of God who makes the words on a page spring to life and inject vitality into our withering lives. Realizing that God is our central source of life—the one who reveals all truth and who occupies the center of Christian theology—we can now turn to the Bible, where God reveals the story of bringing his kingdom into the world.

▶ ▶ ▶ FOR FURTHER READING

- *Praying with the Church* (Brewster, MA: Paraclete Press, 2006), by Scot McKnight
- *The Divine Hours* edited, compiled and with preface by Phyllis Tickle
- *The Divine Hours: Prayers for Springtime: A Manual for Prayer* (New York: Doubleday, 2006)
- *The Divine Hours: Prayers for Summertime* (New York: Doubleday, 2006)
- *The Divine Hours: Prayers for Autumn and Wintertime* (New York: Doubleday, 2006)

- *Experiencing the Depths of Jesus Christ* (Beaumont: The Seed Sowers, 1975), by Jeanne Guyon
- *The Sacred Way: Spiritual Practices for Everyday Life* (Grand Rapids, MI: Zondervan, 2005), by Tony Jones

For additional resources and discussion, see http://inamirror-dimly.com/coffeehouse-theology/chapter-7.

A Web of Theology

This web illustrates the interconnected nature of Christian theology's sources and contexts.

Current chapter topic will be in bold.

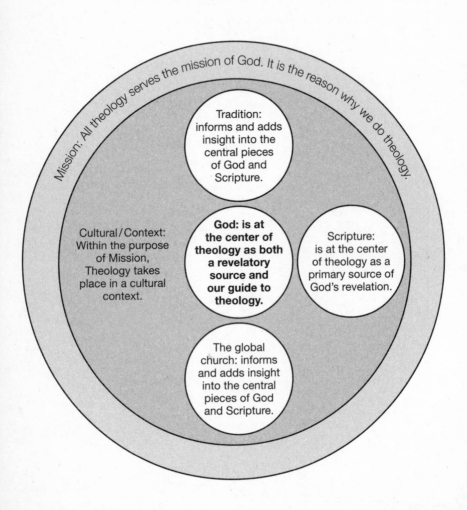

Mission: All theology serves the mission of God. It is the reason why we do theology.

Tradition: informs and adds insight into the central pieces of God and Scripture.

Cultural / Context: Within the purpose of Mission, Theology takes place in a cultural context.

God: is at the center of theology as both a revelatory source and our guide to theology.

Scripture: is at the center of theology as a primary source of God's revelation.

The global church: informs and adds insight into the central pieces of God and Scripture.

Chapter 8

THE BIBLE

Our Primary Source in the Postmodern World

Susanna Clarke's novel *Jonathan Strange and Mr. Norrell* opens upon the Society of Learned Magicians in early nineteenth-century England, that discusses and endlessly debates historical magic — magic which hasn't been seen for hundreds of years. In fact, the newest member of the society is shocked to learn that none of the group's members is able to conjure the simplest of spells. The mysterious but tiresome Mr. Norrell quickly outmatches and outwits the society by bringing to life a series of stone statues in a village church. This fateful act unleashes a series of events that marks the return of magic to England and leads to Norrell's employing Jonathan Strange as his apprentice.

The rules of reality bend under the weight of the two magicians' skills. And with the aid of magic, England gains the edge in its war against the armies of Napoleon. Strange himself ensures victory in Spain and at the crucial Battle of Waterloo. Still, the two magicians part ways because of their different visions for magic. Norrell prefers to keep it bottled up in his study, while Strange spends every moment spreading magic throughout the land. At the climax of the story, the two magicians engage in an earth-shattering struggle that determines the fate of magic in England forever.[1]

Clarke's England provides readers with a powder keg of excitement and possibilities by the story's end. The return of magic to England brings about incredible changes and fulfills the dreams of many. I found it devastating to read the last word because I felt as if I lived in this exciting world of magic, while the bland routines of laundry, cleaning, working, and renovating our home waited for me in the real world. Digging into a magical England connected with a desire to somehow rise above the vanilla contours of life that leave us longing for a taste of something more than what we see.

What if a book unfolded a different and even true story with supernatural possibilities, an alternative to our materialistic, fast-paced, me-first world? As a Christian I can confidently say the Bible does just that. However, as Christians, we often don't treat the Bible as such a book: a coherent, alternative, completely true, relevant story for today. Just imagine if the Bible's stories of miracles, deliverance, and divine intervention seemed more real than the cars we drive, the tables we eat at, or the chairs in our living rooms.

While most Christians hold the Bible in high regard and reverence, we all too easily fall into the trap of classifying it in the reference category. The Bible becomes a repository of religious laws and commands, as well as a collection of bizarre stories that include a talking burning bush, a prophetic donkey, and an assassin's sword swallowed into a king's fat stomach. When critics of the Bible question its truthfulness, I have to wonder if anyone could be clever enough to make up so many fantastic stories—although in light of *Shrek* and its sequels, I'll have to concede the talking donkey part.

What's more, if we don't quite know what to think of the Bible —rules, stories, battles, death, love, miracles—we don't always know why we read it either. We most often read the Bible for spiritual growth and guidance: instructions on how to live and what to believe. These are great reasons to read the Bible, but there is so much more to the story found in Genesis through Revelation.

The Bible is more than theological truths or a book of rules on how to live. In the broadest sense, the Bible tells the alternate story we all search for, a story with ramifications that dramatically revamp how we live. It presents us with God's story: his pursuit of humanity throughout history in spite of disobedience and heartbreak. At center stage stands God, who loves creation and tirelessly works to repair this broken, sin-shattered world through the chosen people. We don't study the Bible just for correct doctrine; we study the Bible in order to know God and to bring his kingdom into our world.

This means that while we live in postmodern times and look at Scripture through a postmodern lens, we ultimately let the story of Scripture define how we live in our world. Whether or not postmodernism calls into question the truth of God, the possibility of miracles, or the existence of meaning in the words of the Bible, Christians join the great cloud of witnesses throughout time who looked to the revelation of God's Word as their primary source for guidance. We believe that we receive God's message for us, that the Holy Spirit manifests his power in our world, and that God's kingdom advances into our lives and the lives of many who don't yet know the Lord.

Even if the postmodern world tells us we'll never quite find all of the truth God reveals, figure out every possible interpretation for Scripture, or achieve complete certainty with our theology, the revelation of Scripture grounds us with the assurance that we indeed know part of the truth, part of the interpretation, and part of God's plan for this world. And these provide enough for us to keep searching for more and growing in the grace and knowledge of our Lord. The narrative of redemption—the coming of God's kingdom—is the true reality that defines our lives, even if we'll never quite understand it completely and always need to continue reading Scripture within our traditions and with Christians from other perspectives.

The Bible provides a God's-eye view of history, while also teaching us about God and the plan for creation. While we can't scientifically prove God's role in writing the Bible beyond the shadow of a doubt, generations of Jews and Christians have regarded the Bible as divinely inspired, setting it aside with special authority as God's revelation. In other words, God revealed himself to a small group of writers, and they consequently wrote according to his revelation (see John 16:12-15; 2 Timothy 3:16; 2 Peter 3:15-16).

Over time, God's people recognized the unique character of these Scriptures in shaping godly Christian communities and possessing strong credentials of apostolic authority (at least in the case of the New Testament). So they viewed these Scriptures as a constant guide in the study of God. With this primary source in hand, we possess a reliable guide that can't be discarded because the consensus of Christians throughout history assures us of its reliability.[2] And while God possesses the capability to speak directly to his people, and the traditions of the church provide helpful guidance, the Bible remains our most constant and reliable source for learning about our Savior and being transformed into God's kind of people.

READING THE BIBLE TODAY

When I married Julie, I wanted the best for her. Being a reasonable man, I thought the best meant making her like me. That's right, she needed to learn the joy and freedom of being very practical, organized, and neat. In my view, you most enjoy life when you find what you like and then just stick to it, not getting wrapped up in new, challenging projects that make a mess of the living room or result in unidentifiable food projects in the refrigerator.

As you might expect, things turned out quite differently than I imagined, with dead flowers hung up to dry in various places, massive canning projects begun, elaborate Indian and Thai meals conjured up from scratch, and the house's not looking so hot. Knowing I wasn't thrilled about the state of our home, Julie tried to keep the place up to my standards but ended up frustrated and miserable.

After a lot of conversation and prayer, we divided the household duties in the following way: I do household maintenance, Julie handles all food purchasing, planning, and preparation, and we both do the laundry. With some of my expectations removed, a fascinating thing happened! The dried out flowers I would throw out were now artistically arranged around candles. We eat some of the best marmalade and applesauce around. Thai food has become one of my favorites, and I find Indian food more appealing than I ever imagined. We now do canning projects together and give jam and marmalade as Christmas presents. The lesson I gleaned: Let go of my expectations for Julie so I can enjoy her as she is. Once I stopped trying to make her into my own image, she had the freedom to blossom as an experimenter, artist, and cook.

We all face similar temptations today to re-create the Bible according to our own tastes and according to the demands of our culture. Christians in the modern age fell to the temptation of interpreting the Bible from one limited perspective that they mistakenly considered universal and binding to all cultures. Now in the postmodern age, Christians run the risk of fragmenting among the diversity of views and cultures in the world, leading to further divisions and a loss of meaningful conclusions from Bible study. In the modern age, Christians latched onto one interpretation to the detriment of other views, while in the postmodern context, we run the risk of losing any kind of footing because we try to travel on too many paths at once. Either way, we run the risk of re-creating the Bible in our own image. This means we face the delicate task of understanding our culture, but also remembering that we sometimes will see only what we want, and ignore the parts that don't fit with our preconceptions.

I see this in my own camp of evangelicals. Many of us Protestants get sweaty palms every time we go through the book of James, praying that James can't really mean that works somehow can achieve salvation. We avoid the messy laws, prophetic oracles of judgment, and mass slaughters of ethnic groups in the Old Testament. A quick dose of Genesis, a good king or two, a heart-warming gospel story about Jesus loving Zacchaeus or some other outcast, a healthy heap of Pauline epistles, and then slam the Bible closed before we inadvertently open it to Revelation, and that's all the Bible we need. I remember with shame telling a professor in college that I wanted to skip a course on the Gospels, because I didn't think they were as important as the Pauline Epistles—as if I could pick and choose between the Gospels and Epistles. We're the product of our history and culture, and to a great extent my love for Paul's letters can be traced right back to the Protestant Reformation that exploded out of the book of Romans. Whether modern or postmodern, Protestant or Catholic, we run the risk of refashioning the Bible into our own image.

In the West, we tend to think of our interpretations as so normal and universal in Bible study that we often call American theology "theology," while we give every other form of theology a qualifier such as "Asian theology" or "African theology." Theologian Dan R. Stiver comments, "While one's location should be considered a strength as well as an unavoidable reality, we have an obligation to dialogue with theologies written from other perspectives."[3] Through this connection with the worldwide church and the various traditions around us, we can begin to step out of our own cultural limitations and see the Spirit of God using Scripture in ways that we could never imagine. In order to be informed of our cultural perspective as Christians, we must be aware of our own limitations and seek out the helpful insights of other Christians. The problem comes when we vigorously defend our own insights and attack the limitations of others. The truth is, because of our limited perspective, we desperately need the insights of the Spirit-led community of believers, Christian traditions, and worldwide Christians when studying the Bible in order to arrive at the most accurate interpretations possible.

While postmodernism might cast doubts on our ability to arrive at any kind of truth we can trust in or apply, contextual theology that maintains a healthy dialogue with culture and these Christian perspectives can provide a helpful alternative to "anything goes" relativism. We can arrive at truth that isn't limited to "what works for me," but rather what works for many Christians listening to the voice of God throughout history and around the world. This kind of theological consensus overcomes the limits of a postmodern world, resulting in truth that speaks to the concerns of our postmodern age, while also clearly proclaiming God's message.

As contextual theologians, we seek to understand God while remaining aware of the limits brought by our own context. With the perspective of postmodernism at our disposal, we need to read the Bible with sensitivity to context, both of the reader and of the passage at hand. This involves a twofold approach that first expands our understanding of our own culture and perspective by including the Spirit, tradition, and global church, and that second, follows up with a collection of resources every theologian should consult from time to time in order to dig deeper into the world of the Bible and to understand the original context of the biblical world. Before we delve into that world, let's look at how a Spirit-directed reading of the Bible works.

THE APOSTLES, SCRIPTURE, AND THE HOLY SPIRIT

While we really can't recreate the conditions under which the apostles Peter and Paul interpreted the Old Testament, several passages in the New Testament indicate that the apostles interpreted them in ways that would make many Christians today uncomfortable. We might not flinch while reading the passages where Peter and Paul make bold new interpretations outside of the original intent of the texts they quote, but can we imagine Christians doing the same today? Keep in mind that many Christian scholars and pastors have learned to study only the context of Scripture, digging into the original meaning and then presenting that exact interpretation for us today.[4] Nothing is wrong with this method; I use it all of the time myself. However, the apostles departed from this method quite dramatically. For example, follow the argument of Paul throughout this excerpt from Galatians that employs a method of interpretation known as allegory:

These things may be taken figuratively, for the women represent two covenants. One covenant is from Mount Sinai and bears children who are to be slaves: This is Hagar. Now Hagar stands for Mount Sinai in Arabia and corresponds to the present city of Jerusalem, because she is in slavery with her children. But the Jerusalem that is above is free, and she is our mother. For it is written:

"Be glad, O barren woman,
who bears no children;
break forth and cry aloud,
you who have no labor pains;
because more are the children of the desolate woman
than of her who has a husband." [Isaiah 54:1]

Now you, brothers, like Isaac, are children of promise. At that time the son born in the ordinary way persecuted the son born by the power of the Spirit. It is the same now. But what does the Scripture say? "Get rid of the slave woman and her son, for the slave woman's son will never share in the inheritance with the free woman's son." [Genesis 21:10] Therefore, brothers, we are not children of the slave woman, but of the free woman. (Galatians 4:24-31)

This passage shows that Paul didn't adhere to a strictly literal interpretation of the Bible. Something compelled Paul to go beyond the original contexts of Isaiah 54 and Genesis 21 to make a statement about the status of Christians under the law. While we might not have any problem with Paul's interpreting Scripture this way, what would we think of Christians who did the same today?

We see a similar phenomenon when Peter preaches to the gathering of Jews during Pentecost in Acts 2. After quoting a rather cryptic passage from the prophet Joel about the Spirit of God being poured out in the last days, Peter goes on to convict his audience of their role in sending Jesus, the Son of God and true Messiah, to his death:

God has raised this Jesus to life, and we are all witnesses of the fact. Exalted to the right hand of God, he has received from the Father the promised Holy Spirit and has poured out what you now see and hear. For David did not ascend to heaven, and yet he said,

"The Lord said to my Lord:
'Sit at my right hand
until I make your enemies
a footstool for your feet.'" [Psalm 110:1]

> "Therefore let all Israel be assured of this: God has made this Jesus, whom you crucified, both Lord and Christ."
>
> When the people heard this, they were cut to the heart and said to Peter and the other apostles, "Brothers, what shall we do?" (Acts 2:32-37)

While Psalm 110, the passage Peter quotes, clearly refers to the Davidic kingship, some strains in the Jewish tradition held to a messianic understanding of the psalm. Peter picks up on this Jewish tradition and artfully links it with Jesus to clearly proclaim the messianic identity of Christ. While we might be slow today to catch the implications of Peter's commentary on Psalm 110, his original listeners immediately grasped its implications and responded with repentance.

In both these cases, Peter and Paul clearly used Scripture outside of its original context in order to make powerful new interpretations. The question is, if the plain meaning of the passages in their original contexts didn't call for the interpretations the two apostles offered, what compelled them to preach and write in such a way? If we believe the Holy Spirit inspired the writing of Paul and the Holy Spirit had just descended on Peter before his sermon, perhaps the Holy Spirit had something to do with this, not to mention a familiarity with the interpretive methods of their times.

Think about this: The two guys we look to as pillars of Christianity used a method of interpreting Scripture that probably wouldn't fly in most congregations today. Can you imagine a pastor saying, "We know the original meaning of this text, but I have a feeling that it really refers to something else." And if someone came on the scene claiming a special revelation that provides a whole new way of interpreting a particular passage of Scripture, who knows what kind of heresy or cult might come to pass? Should we start interpreting the Bible like Peter and Paul—listening to the voice of the Holy Spirit and using the interpretive methods of our times?

Without the illumination the Holy Spirit provides, the words of the Bible can't bring about the truth and life that God desires. Paul stresses the importance of linking the words of Scripture with the work of the Spirit in 2 Corinthians 3. He says that the words of the law by themselves are death,[5] but when Scripture is united with the Spirit, it becomes life to us.

In other words, when we rely on the Spirit to teach and apply Scripture to us, we essentially open ourselves up to the continuing breath of God that brought about the Bible in the first place. Only through the Spirit can the Scriptures bring truth and life. As theologian Kevin J. Vanhoozer notes: "The inspiration of Scripture in the past and the illumination of Scripture in the present are but twin moments of one continuous work of the Holy Spirit."[6]

While we learn from Peter and Paul that the Holy Spirit can sometimes reinterpret a passage of Scripture, we need to figure out a way to do this in our postmodern culture without fragmenting Christians into little islands of doctrine, each hearing God and coming up with personal theologies quite different from everyone else. This means we have both an opportunity to hear God's Spirit afresh, but also the very real danger that we could distort the truth and wreck our theology on the rocks of false doctrines. We navigate these dangers by not abandoning a study of the Bible's context and by listening to the Spirit among Christian community.

THE ROLE OF CHRISTIAN COMMUNITY

Because Jesus promised the Spirit's ministry of revealing truth (see John 16:13), we should read the Bible with an eager expectation for the

Spirit to speak through the words we study. The Holy Spirit takes the words of the Bible and applies them to our lives, forming us into the holy people of God. Theologian and author Stanley Grenz stated, "The Spirit creates the church by speaking through the word. By speaking in and through the biblical text the Spirit brings into being a converted people, that is, a people who forsake their old life so as to inhabit the new, eschatological world centered on Jesus Christ who is the Word."[7] In other words, God creates a new people to partake in God's future rule (eschatological is a formal way of referring to the end times or conclusion of history) in the present. Because as Christians we link to God by the Spirit, and the Bible is the instrument of the Spirit, we can expect the Spirit of God to take an active and (at times) tangible role in leading us through the Scriptures. We don't just read the Bible with the Holy Spirit, we read with the Holy Spirit and the Christian community formed by the Spirit. Though our postmodern world says that truth is hard to find, language is tough to interpret, and our world is too complex to understand, Christians benefit from the ministry of the Holy Spirit among our communities (both local, global, and ancient) to keep us on course toward the truth.

We can stress even more the crucial role of the Spirit in forming Christian community for the purpose of interpreting the Scriptures when we notice that Jesus himself never left a written account of his message. If Jesus had written a book, we probably would have worshipped the book rather than Jesus. Instead of penning a spiritual masterpiece that his followers furiously copied and circulated, Jesus invested a great deal of time in creating a community of followers. Missionary Lesslie Newbigin said, "It is of the essence of the matter that he did not provide us with such a record, but communicated the secret to a community which was then sent out into the world to carry the secret into the life of the world, always reappropriating and reinterpreting it in the light of new circumstances."[8]

As Christians hear the voice of the Spirit in new contexts, our faith communities help keep us on track when interpreting the Bible. As a fruit of the Spirit's work in the world, Christian communities in a variety of forms act as the forum where interpretation and theological reflection occur. While individual Christians should read, study, and meditate on the Bible, we equally need to be in dialogue with a local church gathering. While the Spirit and Scripture serve as powerful elements in the growth of the church, I can't emphasize enough that Spirit-formed Christian community serves as an essential component for interpreting Scripture.

God chooses to entrust a group of people with Scripture and the ongoing guidance of the Holy Spirit. The Bible isn't just a book studied all alone, but a living text animated by the Spirit in the communal life of gathered Christians. Theologians John Franke and Stanley Grenz wrote, "The Bible is the final authority in the church (and hence the norming norm in theology) precisely as the Spirit pours forth further light through the text. Through Scripture, the Spirit continually instructs us as Christ's community in the midst of our life together."[9]

If we want to successfully share the message of God today in both a relevant and prophetic way, our study of Scripture needs the guidance of both the Holy Spirit and our Christian communities. We believe that God reveals truth to us, that our studies will point us toward the truth, and that our fellow believers will aid us in that process. This approach to contextual theology speaks with both relevance and with a prophetic message to our times. While we humbly admit the limitations of our individual perspectives, we look to the Holy Spirit and our Christian communities to keep us on track. Theologian Trevor Hart reminded us, "Good theology . . . is the disciplined and critical reflection of the community of faith upon the gospel entrusted to it."[10] We can't presume to correctly interpret the Scriptures on a consistent basis unless we share our lives with the people of God, dialoguing with them and allowing them to correct or affirm our reflections on God.[11] If we want to understand God today, God's Spirit and our communities will be central in this process.

For example, I've found dialogue with a variety of Christians to be particularly helpful in sorting out how to interpret passages of Scripture related to women in ministry,[12] a topic that is particularly sensitive for many Christians. Some verses in Scripture seem to prohibit women from speaking at Christian gatherings or holding any kind of authority over men (see 1 Timothy 2:9-15; 1 Corinthians 14:26-40; and 1 Corinthians 11:2-16). Christians apply these verses in a variety of ways. Some churches allow women to speak provided they don't explicitly teach on a passage of Scripture.

Allowing women to teach requires some tricky interpretation of the Bible. The crux of the matter is how we read these restrictions. Are these prohibitions binding for all time or commands that relate to particular situations? My own views were significantly shaped by reading Scripture along with dialoguing with Christians from a variety of perspectives. I used to believe that women shouldn't teach men or hold positions of authority over men in church, until I read a book at my in-laws' place and had a few key discussions with various fellow believers. I can't even remember the title of that book, but the author said he had supported women in ministry ever since the Holy Spirit spoke directly to him about Paul's declaration that there is neither male nor female in Christ (see Galatians 3:26-29).

While this rattled my thinking about women in ministry, the real knockout blow came from witnessing the way God used my mother-in-law in prison ministry and in ministry to others. What can you say when God speaks very clearly through a woman in the ministry? When you look at the people touched by women in ministry, you will find a virtual landslide of Christians from a variety of backgrounds and regions who all support interpreting the Scriptures related to women in ministry as temporal commands.

I thought through these verses in seminary and did extensive research, but only through dialogue with a variety of Christians did my theology change.

Of course when we gather together to reflect on God, we should undertake substantial study ahead of time. Interpreting the Bible is not a matter of following a crowd, but carefully studying Scripture in dialogue with Christians who are doing the same. So let's look at some practical ways we can study Scripture.

BASIC TOOLS OF BIBLE STUDY

We certainly want to understand the influences of our own cultures and the importance of the Holy Spirit and Christian community when studying the Bible in the postmodern context. But we also need to actually open the Good Book and try to figure out what's going on. That means we need to dig into the world of the Bible and try to understand the original context of Scripture using commentaries, Bible dictionaries, and other Bible study resources. We need these tools because Bible study is an intersection of who we are and the original context of the Bible. The only limits on how much we can find out about the Bible's context are Internet access, time, money, and shelf space. Keep in mind that many churches, Christian colleges, and seminaries have extensive collections of study materials available, so you might not always need to make a major purchase.

I need to note that most of what I share here isn't all that new. While theology blogs and some of the Web pages with information about global Christians might be new to you, I'm not going to unveil any huge surprises or secret tools for studying the Bible. In fact, some of this information about different Bible translations, the original languages, commentaries, and Bible dictionaries might feel almost mundane and out of place in a book that urges you to take some bold steps into forming and doing contextual theology. However, while we might use many of the same tools we've always used, as contextual theologians, we now have an increased awareness of the ways our own context influences our interpretation of the Bible's world.

For example, as an American, I've never lived under a military occupation by a foreign power. After moving out of my parents' home, I've done pretty much what I wanted to within the parameters of the law. However, when I began to pay attention to the context of the Gospels, I noticed that Jesus' ministry takes place within a politically charged world of military occupation. The Roman rulers had militarily crushed the Jews, brutally suppressed insurrections, and then done their best to appease the Jews by rebuilding their temple — the very one where Jesus removed the moneylenders. Because I'm aware of my own context, I readily recognize that I'm particularly ill-suited for understanding this facet of the Gospels. This awareness makes me all the more keen to study Bible dictionaries and commentaries to uncover as much as I can about this important backdrop for Jesus' ministry.

As our world meets with the Bible's world, we have the difficult task of understanding events and literature far removed from our own time. The following tools can help contextual theologians bridge that gap.

Bible Translations

Looking at Scripture through our postmodern lens, we can see that these sacred words give us truth and that we can interpret them with relative certainty even if our knowledge is limited and we need additional perspectives. One way we can overcome the uncertainty and complexity of the language of an ancient text translated into today's language and culture is to consult multiple translations.

You can search nearly every version of the Bible online, so you only need to own one or two translations of the Bible for regular reading and study. Access to the Internet unlocks almost every version of the Bible on sites such as www.biblegateway.com. Many Christians use the New International Version (NIV) and Today's New International Version (TNIV), two translations I often use for study. Although a brief controversy surrounded the TNIV's release,[13] the translation doesn't compromise the Greek and Hebrew originals.[14] The NIV and TNIV translations are accurate yet easy to read, which means the translators took a more interpretive approach rather than translating word by word.

The English Standard Version (ESV) and New American Standard Bible (NASB) lean toward greater accuracy on a word-by-word basis, but this sacrifices some readability. Many Bible scholars use the New Revised Standard Version (NRSV), while many Christians familiar with the Internet enjoy the NET Bible (available for free at www.bible.org), which provides extensive translation and study notes.[15]

I also regularly read the New Living Translation (NLT), which sometimes provides a more interpretive translation than other versions. Still, I find that the NLT offers both an accurate and extremely easy to read translation of the Bible. The NLT makes it easier to read large sections of the Bible in one sitting, which I believe is important for acquainting ourselves with the whole story of Scripture. Eugene Peterson's translation, *The Message*, is a contemporary version that also enables readers to easily read through large sections of the Bible, providing readers with a good general sense of entire biblical books.[16]

Commentaries, Dictionaries, and Other Large Books

Commentaries and Bible dictionaries are particularly significant for contextual theology because they help us find disconnects between our culture and the culture of the Bible. The more we know about the world of Scripture, the more we can fill in the gaps between our times and ancient times. Without this important leg of our theology, we just hop along with knowledge of who we are, but can't really run with a balanced understanding of the disconnects between ourselves and the context of Scripture.

Commentaries provide at least three services: analysis of the original language, examination of the cultural context, and explanation of the biblical text. Not all commentaries provide all three of these. In fact, most don't. Some commentaries, especially the scholarly volumes such as the ANCHOR BIBLE series, usually aren't written by professing Christians but rather religion scholars who are interested in determining how the books of the Bible were written, rather than what the finished books have to say. So before you shell out hundreds of dollars on commentaries and book shelves, try to analyze each volume to find out what it promises.

Perhaps the most comprehensive series around is the WORD BIBLICAL COMMENTARY (Thomas Nelson), but many pastors also enjoy the EXPOSITOR'S BIBLE COMMENTARY (Zondervan). My personal favorite for the New Testament is N. T. Wright's series with titles such as *Matthew for Everyone*, *Mark for Everyone*, and *Paul for Everyone* (Westminster). Wright provides just enough contextual and linguistic analysis, while delivering a double serving of explanation of biblical passages. While no one series of commentaries stands out as superior to all others—in fact, the volumes in each series will vary in usefulness based on the authors' expertise—several commentaries are worth considering for everyday study, such as the following: INTERPRETATION BIBLE COMMENTARY (Westminster), THE NEW AMERICAN COMMENTARIES (B&H), *The New International Bible Commentary* (Zondervan), THE NIV APPLICATION COMMENTARY (Zondervan), and THE PILLAR COMMENTARY series (Eerdmans).[17]

Another popular tool for Bible study is a Bible dictionary. These works can be as small as one volume, such as the *New International Bible Dictionary* by J. D. Douglas (Grand Rapids, MI: Zondervan, 1987), or can extend to six or more such as the *Anchor Bible Dictionary* (New York: Bantam, Dell Doubleday). A one-volume work is probably all that most students of the Bible need. For those who want an in-depth study tool, one of the best is the series of dictionaries by InterVarsity Press which include *Dictionary of Jesus and the Gospels*, *Dictionary of Paul and His Letters*, and so on. Other large books used for Bible study include a Bible atlas and *Vine's Expository Dictionary of Old and New Testament Words* (Nashville, TN: Thomas Nelson, 1997), but with the resources available online, these are unnecessary purchases for those familiar with using the Internet.

Commentaries and dictionaries provide the best scholarly perspectives available on passages of Scripture, and these scholarly voices make important contributions to theology by providing not only analysis of the text's language and cultural setting but also helpful insight on how exactly to interpret Scripture. The insights found in commentaries and dictionaries remind us that the Bible has a cultural setting all its own that we must consider in addition to the influences of our context on our interpretations.

Free Online Tools

While consulting a seminary, church, or university library might be one of the best ways to find free Bible study materials, a surprising number of resources exist online. For starters on www.zoecarnate. com, also known as Sites Unseen, Mike Morrell and Philip Scriber have done an outstanding job of collecting Christian resources from all over the Web—especially documents from Christian history and other websites—that will help any student of the Bible. They provide links to some of the best theology blogs. One of the most helpful parts of a blog is the list of that author's favorite blogs, making the possibilities for resources and conversation partners practically limitless. Additional theology resources can be found at my blog http://inamirrordimly.com and at www.bible.org.

Keep in mind that you can find an almost endless stream of resources out there. King Solomon didn't know anything about blogs and websites when he said that the writing of books is endless. We now virtually—in the most literal way you can be virtual—are swimming in information. As you seek out Bible study tools online, take it slow. Don't open too many sites at once. Forget about the vast possibilities unfolding before you and master a few good sites before seeking out additional bins of Christian information.

Online resources hold particular value for contextual theology because they make the perspectives of Christian theologians, lay ministers, and pastors available. We can find a variety of views on topics and passages of Scripture at no cost and with relative ease, enabling us to broaden our interpretations beyond our limited horizons, taking in the truth God has revealed to Christians around the world who are studying Scripture just like we are.

Biblical Languages

Having taken an extra year of Greek and a sufficient number of classes in Hebrew, I can safely say that while the original languages of the Bible provide immense help and can greatly benefit Bible study, they won't make or break anyone's walk with the Lord. Some of the greatest saints throughout church history couldn't even read the Bible in their own language, let alone in the originals.

Knowing the original languages of the biblical texts doesn't provide a super-spiritual key to the Bible. Access to some *secret* aspect of a Greek word doesn't unlock powerful, life-changing meanings in a text. Yes, sometimes a subtle nuance brings a text to life or adds some helpful emphasis. Of course, a good translation from the original languages can make all the difference between Christianity and heresy; for example, our translation of John 1:1 reads, "the Word was God," whereas the Jehovah's Witnesses render it, "the Word was a god." Just a subtle article such as *a* can make a huge difference,[18] so we can be thankful for the translators who carefully present the words of Scripture to us in our native languages.

However, if you have interest, Greek and Hebrew aren't as hard to learn as you might think. Just a year of study often brings many students to a reasonable proficiency level, which can be enough when combined with the many language tools available. Two great language programs for the computer, *Gramcord* and *Logos*, each provide a translation and parsing by simply moving the pointer over each word. These programs, which carry a price tag in the $200 range, make continuing use of biblical languages possible for pastors and lay persons alike.

STUDYING THE BIBLE BOOK BY BOOK

Now that we've been on a swirling tour of our context, grappled with God's role, and piled our desks with reference books, it's time to actually study the Bible. We generally study the Bible for two reasons: for spiritual growth and to answer theological questions. Both yield theology in their own right. The first aims for spiritual growth in the church; the second focuses on joining God's kingdom mission in our world.

No matter what the reason, I find it helpful to approach the Bible on a book-by-book basis, quickly reading through a book with the New Living Translation or *The Message* before taking additional study time in a more literal translation. Having the big picture can help sort through the smaller bits.

For example, early in my Christian life, I became obsessed with the issue of faith versus works. Everywhere I looked, I found passages that stressed the importance of having faith and not relying on our own works for salvation. My Bible from this time reveals highlighting and underlining of every verse even vaguely related to this pet topic.

I particularly latched onto the first half of the book of Romans (Romans 1–8), but conveniently forgot the second half of the book, which details the reconciliation of Jews and Gentiles in Christ. Instead of reading this epistle as a conceptual whole—treating it like any other letter—I chose to read it like an encyclopedia and focused on what I considered the highlights. My scattered approach to the Bible missed out on the larger themes of each book because I had one particular topic in mind. As a result of my narrow focus, I always found verses to support my topic wherever I looked.

After reading through a book of the Bible or at least reading a summary from a study Bible's introduction, choose a schedule that works for you. One professor from my seminary suggested taking a few days in the week to do in-depth Bible study, while Neil Cole, a prominent church planter, strongly advocates reading through at least five chapters of Scripture each day.[19] I enjoy picking up a book such as N. T. Wright's commentary series on the New Testament and using it for my Bible study times. Your goals will determine how far you expand each study with additional resources such as dictionaries.

As a student of the Bible, aim to grasp a clear picture of your own context, and then study with an eye to the setting of each passage. As the Spirit of God speaks, you'll draw conclusions and gain new insights. Still, when these conclusions begin forming into a theology or doctrine, your work isn't quite done.

The truth is that we're not the first or only ones to study the Bible and to shape theology. The church has been up to the same thing for two thousand years, and Christians all over the world are studying the Bible as well. Both of these sources lend insight and direction. While not as authoritative as the Bible itself, these sources can save us from making the same mistake Christians in the past made, as well as offer views that we'll never have from our vantage point in history and culture.

We'll look at these other sources in depth in the next two chapters.

▶ ▶ ▶ FOR FURTHER READING

- *Bible Doctrine: Essential Teachings of the Christian Faith* (Grand Rapids, MI: Zondervan, 1999), by Wayne Grudem
- *The Essential IVP Reference Collection: The Complete Electronic Bible Study Resource* (Downers Grove, IL: InterVarsity, 2003), Version 2.0 on CD-ROM
- *Is There a Meaning in This Text? The Bible, the Reader, and the Morality of Literary Knowledge* (Grand Rapids, MI: Zondervan, 1998), by Kevin J. Vanhoozer
- *The Art of Reading Scripture* (Grand Rapids, MI: Eerdmans, 2003), by Ellen F. Davis and Richard B. Hays
- *Engaging Scripture: A Model for Theological Interpretation* (Malden, MA: Wiley-Blackwell, 1998), by Stephen E. Fowl
- *Words of Delight: A Literary Introduction to the Bible* (Grand Rapids, MI: Baker, 1993), by Leland Ryken
- THE GOSPEL ACCORDING TO THE OLD TESTAMENT series (Phillipsburg, NJ: P & R Publishing)
- *Jesus and the Victory of God* (Minneapolis, MN: Augsburg Fortress, 1997), by N. T. Wright

- The FOR EVERYONE series of New Testament commentaries (Louisville, KY: Westminster), by N. T. Wright
- *International Standard Bible Encyclopedia* (Grand Rapids, MI: Eerdmans)

For additional resources and discussion, see http://inamirrordimly .com/coffeehouse-theology/chapter-8.

A Web of Theology

This web illustrates the interconnected nature of Christian theology's sources and contexts.

Current chapter topic will be in bold.

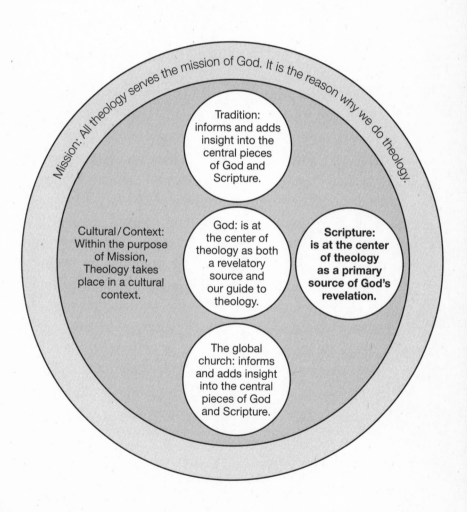

Mission: All theology serves the mission of God. It is the reason why we do theology.

Tradition: informs and adds insight into the central pieces of God and Scripture.

Cultural/Context: Within the purpose of Mission, Theology takes place in a cultural context.

God: is at the center of theology as both a revelatory source and our guide to theology.

Scripture: is at the center of theology as a primary source of God's revelation.

The global church: informs and adds insight into the central pieces of God and Scripture.

Chapter 9

THE TRADITION OF THE CHURCH

Keeping Us Grounded

While home from college one summer, I walked past the greeting cards, booming music videos, and stacked shelves of Bibles in search of what I thought was the most important section of my local Christian bookstore: the Bible commentaries. I had already locked on to ministry as a calling for my life — what could be better than a full-time job teaching people about Jesus? My future plans included seminary, so I desired Bible dictionaries, commentaries, and other imposing reference books that would one day loom large in my study, letting everyone in my congregation know that I have a seminary education and — watch out — I know how to use it!

The selection of commentaries was a bit thin at the bookstore. I didn't see any of the commentaries that I knew and loved from my university's library. Then I came across one series of paperback commentaries. I picked up a volume on the gospel of Mark and noted that the price was right and that the author had a lot to say about each section of Scripture. I knew the author of the commentary was a famous theologian whose name also appeared in a popular comic strip: John Calvin.

PAPISTS AND CALVIN WITHOUT HOBBES

That night, as I dove into the teachings of Calvin, I was quickly thrown for a loop. He obsessed about these people he called "Papists," denouncing them at every turn. I didn't recall that Papists even showed up in the Gospels, and I failed to catch on to who they were. When I couldn't take it anymore, I did a little research and discovered that "Papists" is another name for Catholics. It all became clear: John Calvin lived during the Reformation, and he thought of the Roman Catholic Church—with its corruption and oppression of Reformers of that time—as the primary enemy of Christians in his camp. When Calvin read the Gospels, he naturally saw strong applications for his relations with Catholics—something he liberally sprinkled throughout his commentary, to the point where I could hardly follow his reasoning.

Apparently I wasn't ready for historical theology at that point in my life; I ended up selling Calvin's commentary on Amazon.com and probably bought a CD instead.

Even though I didn't spend much time with Calvin's commentary and I didn't quite catch on to his thoughts, in retrospect, I believe that my purchase was very formative in my growth as a Christian theologian—if you can believe it. Calvin showed me that we're all stuck in a particular time and place and that we must apply theology appropriately.

This local, temporary nature of theology shows why we must continually shape and reshape it. I'm sure that our theological beliefs will look strange fifty, one hundred, and especially two hundred years from now. Calvin's commentary showed me that context dictates how we read and interpret the Bible, a challenge we must face today.

INCLUDING TRADITION IN OUR WEB OF THEOLOGY

When we approach theology, we see a rich and varied tradition, indicating that we're not the first ones to take a swing at this. Two thousand years of Christianity has produced a large crop of theologians. While some reside on an obscure shelf in a dusty seminary library, a few—such as Origen, Tertullian, Augustine, Aquinas, Erasmus, Luther, and Calvin—stand as giants in the history of Christianity and loom over many of our dearest doctrines today. These doctrines and teachings play an important role in our expanding web of Christian theology. God and Scripture stand fixed in the center, with the traditions of the church just slightly outside. Some traditions end up closer to the center than others—while some are heresies and not even in the web. But the vast majority of the traditions found in Christianity's history have something to teach us about theology and context.

We owe the historic church a great deal. Whether or not we use icons, baptize infants, believe in the joined divinity and humanity of Christ, or recite a creed every Sunday, all of these practices find their roots in the work of the historic church. Heresies don't declare themselves as such, so a group of Christians at one point in time had to decide that certain doctrines didn't belong in the fold. While God doesn't change, Christians constantly face new challenges that result in fresh reflections on God in changing cultures and periods of history. Theologian Tony Jones speaks of orthodoxy (the accepted doctrines of Christianity) as an event: "*Orthodoxy happens* when human beings get together and practice it (talk about God, worship God, pray to God, write books about God, etc.)."[1]

Today's church reflects a tumultuous history of shaping key doctrines in the face of persecution and heresies, but as a result the church has preserved true traditions, weeded out corruption during the Reformation and Council of Trent, and explained the Bible in an age of skepticism. As we try to determine what's orthodox or truly Christian in today's culture, we can learn a great deal from the traditions of the historic church that faced similar challenges long before us.

THE ROLE OF TRADITION IN CONTEXTUAL THEOLOGY

As we work toward developing theology that looks at our faith through a postmodern lens, we'll find that Christian tradition provides an essential contribution. These traditions reveal the grand narrative of God's people throughout time as they struggled to embody him in a particular time and place. As we look back at the shifts within the church throughout history, the influences of culture and philosophy on Christian doctrine become apparent. However, we also need to make sure we reference tradition after we study Scripture itself.

Although not on the same authoritative level as Scripture, Christian tradition provides an essential reference point in forming theology.[2] The traditions that withstand the test of time prove their worth. As we form theology in the postmodern context, we enrich our faith by including the diverse voices heard throughout history and paying particular attention to the truths that have always been a part of the Christian community.

The early church fathers distilled the most essential collection of traditions into the rule of faith, later rewritten in form of the Apostles' Creed.[3] As the church's beliefs changed over time, many Christians expanded their conception of tradition to encompass what they called the Great Tradition. Theologian Roger Olson describes this as "mere Christianity — the consensus beliefs held in common by the early church fathers and the Reformers of the sixteenth century as expressed in common by the ecumenical creeds and Reformation confessions of faith."[4] Beyond these essential creeds that formed the church into what it is today, theologians and doctrines emerged with varying levels of value when compared with the Great Tradition. Still, even the most blatant heresy holds a lesson for the church about theology and culture.

For example, in the early church there were some who rejected the doctrine of the Trinity — a concept that is to Christianity what apple pie is to America. A popular theologian named Arius gained a substantial following at the end of the third century and in the early years of the fourth century. Among other doctrines, Arius taught that Jesus didn't exist eternally with God and that, in fact, God created Jesus. Not just intellectual elites adopted Arianism but entire congregations throughout the Christian church accepted his claims.

In fact, the views of Arius became so popular in the eastern Mediterranean region that Emperor Constantine intervened and ordered a council. During the Council of Nicaea in 325, Christian leaders held up the views of Arius against the Bible and the teachings of other church fathers, resulting in their conclusion that Arianism was heresy. The council found this heresy so serious that those who followed Arius were ordered to agree that the Father, Spirit, and Son were one substance and one person. If they didn't agree, they faced exile — not one of the finer moments for Christian unity, but you at least can understand what they believed to be at stake. Those attending this council wrote the Nicene Creed, arguably one of the most important works of doctrine in the history of the church. The Nicene Creed helps today's Christian church distinguish itself from groups such as the Latter Day Saints, who claim that God is united in purpose, but not in substance — or simply put, that Jesus is not

God in the same way that the Father is God.

Throughout history, the church has studied Scripture in light of church traditions, listened to the leading of the Holy Spirit, and then acted accordingly in a particular time and place. The doctrine of the Trinity stands as an example of one tradition that is now an essential dogma of the church. Although none of the New Testament writers explicitly uses the words *trinity* or *triune*, the early church best described the God of the Bible as a trinity: Father, Son, and Holy Spirit. Thanks to their careful decision, the Trinity holds its rightful place as a central doctrine of Christianity.

When we understand that this debate became a defining moment for Christianity—one that could have significantly changed our faith—we understand that our past not only shapes what we believe but it also sets the limits for truth in a postmodern world. In other words, the Trinity stands as a central dogma of Christianity, so any interpretation of Scripture that calls it into question should be scrutinized very closely. We use our Christian tradition today as a guide for interpreting the Bible and forming contextual theology.

THE VALUE OF TRADITION

While some traditions handed down to the church were only useful in a particular time and place, Christian tradition—both the Great Tradition and some lesser traditions—plays a vital role in guiding the church in the forming of theology. Tradition helps us avoid the mistakes of the past and gives shape to the doctrines we hold as most important. Even the heresies that appear to be new often popped up previously as false doctrines in the church. For example, the theory about the humanity of Jesus and his marriage to Mary Magdalene found in author Dan Brown's book *The Da Vinci Code* is a stylized version of the divinity debates surrounding Jesus in the third and fourth centuries, as well as a heretical book known as the gospel of Thomas from the first or second centuries. However, this time, the mass media of our culture helped spread the false message.

In *The Da Vinci Code*, Robert Langdon and Sophie Neveu discuss the Holy Grail with Sir Leigh Teabing while waiting for the police to arrive and renew the action and suspense. Teabing presents an alternate history of Christianity, one that makes the heretics the heroes. Neveu is startled to learn some different views from her new scholarly friends, who say that Jesus was really just a man and that Mary Magdalene was his wife. They also claim that Constantine declared Jesus divine just to consolidate power, and Christians have ever since remained hostile to the keepers of these secrets.

Without a grounding in early church traditions, our faith might be rocked by these scandalous claims. In light of Christian tradition, though, Teabing overplayed his hand when recounting history. For example, keep in mind that immediately prior to the rule of Constantine many Christians died and others were marginalized for their faith in Christ, especially during Diocletian's persecution from 303–311. Though Constantine may have made Christianity a legitimate, if not state religion, Teabing imagines a church with tremendous power and influence in the fourth century: a point that is far from certain. To say that Constantine, fresh off his victory on the battlefield, sought to consolidate his rule by aligning himself with a group that had recently suffered a bloody, divisive persecution strays toward fiction rather than fact.[5]

While Constantine may have wanted to end the theological bickering in his empire, and he certainly did much to advance Christianity as the state religion, the crisis surrounding the divinity of Jesus stemmed less from political maneuvers and more from the limitations of Greek philosophy picked up by Christian thinkers who insisted that Jesus was merely the highest of God's creations and not truly God. When Christians met to figure out the exact way to word the divinity of Christ, they found that the consistent apostolic witness testified to Jesus' being fully God and fully man and that any doubt cast on the divinity of Christ by a few bishops did not match the historical consensus of the church. In fact, the majority were appalled when they learned more about this new teaching calling Jesus' divinity into question. In the end, Constantine may have sped up the process for the sake of political stability, but the divinity of Jesus was a consistent dogma that the church had always upheld, whether enduring persecution or political perks.

When we ground ourselves in our traditions, we find ourselves in a much better position not just to study Scripture but to confront false teachings and to answer the questions that come up when we share the gospel. Instead of offering one limited perspective on an issue, such as the divinity of Christ, which critics have recently cast into doubt again, we can look to the testimony of Christians before us to strengthen our faith and our positions. The truth doesn't rest on what works for you or me, but on what has worked for hundreds of years and continues to work today: the risen life of Christ our Savior changing lives and holding fast no matter what doubts arise.

Looking at the past and present challenges to the divinity of Christ also reminds us that Christian traditions help us understand the limits that culture can impose on theology. If the separation of spirit and matter made the simultaneous humanity and divinity of Christ a tough pill to swallow in ancient Greece, we should keep in mind that our own culture will try to impose limitations on truth and the reliability of our interpretations. Theologians Stanley Grenz and John Franke provide a helpful summary of how tradition can function in contextual theology today:

These past creeds, confessions, and theological formulations
are not binding in and of themselves. They are helpful as
they provide insight into the faith of the church in the past
and as they make us aware of the presuppositions of our
context. . . . Moreover, they must always and continually be
tested by the norm of canonical Scripture.[6]

This is important to remember in light of our postmodern
context, where we can expect presuppositions and bias. By studying the mistakes and triumphs of our theological heritage, we stand
a greater chance of catching our own preconceived notions and
cultural errors, as well as creating opportunities to right the wrongs
of the past.

Of course, integrating tradition into our web of theology represents tricky business, as we try to balance the authority of Scripture
with insights from the past that shape who we are. Theologian Kevin
J. Vanhoozer points out, "Not even the scientific method can free us
from our particular, and limited, historical horizons. Yet it is precisely
these horizons that connect us to the past, for it is the past that
shapes who we are today."[7] So while an expression of Christianity
in postmodern times might not hold the Bible as the *only* source
for theological reflection, Scripture remains the *primary source* or
what scholars call the "norming norm."[8] In other words, no historical interpretation of Scripture can claim a place of supremacy over
Scripture itself. As theologian Dan R. Stiver wrote, "The implication
for theology is that we begin with a text, experience, or tradition that
has already grasped us, which is then critically examined and further
reappropriated. In other words, we recognize that we do not start
from scratch or first build a foundation but begin where we and the
church are."[9] As history moves forward, language and culture will
prompt Christians to interpret the Bible in new ways in light of the

changing world. However, we can always look to our traditions that not only shaped our beliefs, but that continue to guide how we read and interpret the Bible.

VIEWS OF CHRISTIAN TRADITION

Although I believe that Christian tradition should be the next step *after* consulting Scripture for our theology, other perspectives exist today regarding the use of Christian tradition. For example, some independent evangelicals pay little attention to historic theology, believing the Holy Spirit and Scripture are sufficient to bring believers to the truth. On the other end of the spectrum, the Catholic and Greek Orthodox churches rely heavily on Christian tradition. I hope to steer a course that includes the best of Christian tradition in our theology but remains sensitive to the primary place reserved for Scripture.

During my fourth semester of Greek in college, I spent six steamy summer weeks baking in the Indiana farmland, writing a commentary on a small portion of Ephesians. Each student selected a different crop of verses from the book — few sections exceeded seven verses — and created commentaries that often ran longer than twenty double-spaced pages. Besides the grammatical tools at our disposal, the assignment required interacting with every available modern commentary and then drawing our own conclusions. In the midst of these commentaries, we briefly touched on snippets of Christian tradition, but these sources rarely influenced our papers. However, one student stood out as the exception.

A student of the Greek Orthodox denomination refused to follow modern commentators or engage in lengthy exegesis that would lead to his own conclusions. He stalwartly clung to the church fathers and only included these sacred volumes in his research. While the rest of us didn't exactly do our best to understand where he was coming from, he wouldn't consider the value of grammatical and historical analysis provided in today's commentaries. Looking back, I now see how sad it was that those of us with an evangelical background were so far removed from this student's experience. We certainly had a lot to teach one another, but we stood at opposite ends of a vast divide, neither truly listening to the other.

It's easy for Christians at opposite ends of the spectrum to simplify and dismiss each other's views. Yet if we truly listen to one another, we have a lot more in common than we might suspect. Of course, Christians should never go so far as to say that all truth is relative, yet the postmodern perspective—which values diversity and acknowledges the limits of local knowledge—makes it possible to see the merit in other points of view, especially those from other denominations and historic traditions. This creates space to discover more truth, not less. Acknowledging complexity and the limits of our own knowledge allows Christians from various backgrounds to agree on disagreeing, while listening to and learning from one another.

In fact, I see how the Catholic view of Scripture and tradition makes a lot of sense, even if I don't agree with it. Catholics, and to a certain degree Eastern Orthodox Christians, believe:

> Scripture and tradition cannot be separated and that
> Scripture is the God-inspired creation of the church as it
> was led to select the canonical books by the Holy Spirit.
> Tradition is, then, the entire process of God's Spirit speak-
> ing to and within the church—first through the apostles
> and then through the bishops who succeeded them and
> through the councils of the church and through Scripture
> and through the faithful people of God in prayer, worship,
> and witness.[10]

This perspective is valuable because the Bible didn't just fall out of the sky and present itself as God's Word. A group of finite and fallible Christians decided that certain writings possessed more apostolic authority and were more useful than others. At a council, this group canonized the Bible we have today. So if the Bible was essentially compiled by the church, then it's not too far-fetched to say that Scripture and tradition are inseparably joined together.

We can't afford to ignore our traditions, especially the Great Tradition: the creeds and confessions in our Christian history. As theologians John Franke and Stanley Grenz note, "Because we are members of this continuous historical community, the theological tradition of the church must be a crucial component in the construction of our contemporary theological statements, so that we might maintain our theological or confessional unity with the one church of Jesus Christ."[11] In many ways, the historical church produced us and we share fellowship with the same Lord. So we shouldn't cut ourselves off from this significant part of the church.

Although we shouldn't be afraid to arrive at our own conclusions while studying Scripture, we definitely can learn from our traditions when they speak directly to our topic of study. Of course, we can't limit our views to the doctrines of historic Christians, because they were just as likely as we are to make mistakes. So we must reevaluate some of their beliefs, especially the conclusions that don't have the backing of Christians from a variety of traditions and over a long period of time. Our traditions keep us grounded in the essentials that have endured throughout time, provide additional perspectives that help us overcome our own limitations in the postmodern context, and offer examples of the limitations of culture on theologians.

ENDING UP ON THE WRONG SIDE

The halls of history are lined with stories that should throw up red flags for how we read and interpret the Bible. Christians can especially learn a great deal about biblical interpretation from the Essenes at Qumran, a sect of Jews who wrote the Dead Sea Scrolls at a time roughly contemporary with Jesus.[12] During a semester in Jerusalem, I read through most of the Dead Sea Scrolls—copies of biblical documents, commentaries on Scripture, and regulations for community life made during the first century—including the Community Rule and several Scripture commentaries.

The Essenes were a separatist community that gave themselves completely to ritual purity and study of Scripture. They were apocalyptic in that they expected the Messiah to arrive very soon, bringing judgment to everyone but them because they were the chosen sons of light. They especially hated the Pharisees and Sadducees who worked with the Roman occupation to a certain degree, which earned them the title "smooth talkers" or "the talkers who like smooth things."[13] This derogatory statement meant something akin to corrupt and lying.

The Essene Community Rule provides an interesting, if somewhat strange, read. In their Scripture commentaries, which seem tedious and torturous at times, a writer shares a short piece of Scripture and then follows with the signature line, "The interpretation is . . ." After a while, I picked up on the pattern. Typically, anything bad in a passage of Scripture would befall the smooth talkers, while anything good belonged to the faithful sons of light.

Even though I'm amused by the self-righteousness of the Essenes and their obsessive optimism about the sons of light, I can't help thinking of the way I (and many other Christians) read the Bible today. When Jesus says, "Woe to you, Korazin! Woe to you, Bethsaida! For if the miracles that were performed in you had been performed in Tyre and Sidon, they would have repented long ago, sitting in sackcloth and ashes" (Luke 10:13), I think to myself, *Yeah guys, really, shape up.* I can also see applying this passage to the masses of people who ignore God. But when I realize that Jesus said these words to Jews who were supposed to recognize their Savior, I grasp that this warning isn't aimed at the world, but at Christians, who should recognize Jesus when he comes. I know I've been skeptical of God and his power, and I've even been downright indifferent about Jesus sometimes in the midst of my busy life. So, in reality, maybe we're not so different from the Essenes.

As we consider tradition in our effort to form theology in our postmodern culture, we can avoid the trap the Essenes fell into by comparing what we know about ourselves and the way we interpret Scripture with believers who have gone before us. Like the Essenes, we easily assume that all the blessings are for us, while we ignore the warnings. Christians from other points in history provide an escape from the limits of our perspective. This might involve reading a passage of Scripture and comparing our findings with those of another believer from a different point in time, or we might choose to read a book or article about our traditions just to increase our general knowledge—and then reap the benefits at a later point.

I don't know about you, but I squirm a bit in my comfortable life when I read Jesus' saying about the rich people and the eye of the needle: "Again I tell you, it is easier for a camel to go through the eye of a needle than for a rich man to enter the kingdom of God" (Matthew 19:24). Compared to most of the world, I'm a rich man. So, as a wealthy American who reads the words of Jesus, I go on the defensive: "Oh, come on, there are tons of people with more money than us, and we also have student loan debt!" In other words, I thought I had effectively passed the "eye of the needle" competition: "Look, God, no wealth here."

That's where St. Francis of Assisi stepped in. I picked up a book about Francis and Clare of Assisi called *Light in the Dark Ages* (Brewster, MA: Paraclete, 2007) and I found a challenge to my American perspective, a view from Christian tradition regarding the application of Matthew 19. While I'm not advocating for Christians to precisely model their lives after Francis, he does put things into perspective. Francis came from a wealthy family, but over time God gnawed at his conscience, creating a love for the poor. He didn't "marry lady poverty" by eloping, but became compassionate for the poor over the course of a long-term courtship that began with offering his fine clothes to a destitute knight, regularly emptying his pockets at church, wearing the clothes of a beggar, and even going so far as kissing a man with leprosy—a disease everyone believed could be contracted through contact. Francis eventually surrendered his family's dreams for him in order to carry out the work of God among the poor, choosing the kingdom of God over any hindrance.

So I return to Matthew 19, where I'm trying to figure out just how hard it is for me to enter God's kingdom. I know where my next meal will come from, I have shelter, I have a job, and I have a little disposable income. To make matters worse, I live in a very materialistic society obsessed with growth, getting ahead, and owning a slice of the pie, otherwise known as the American Dream. The American Dream easily crowds out God's kingdom dream, and by comparing myself to Francis of Assisi—something I don't do every day, by the way—I can see this in stark relief. Thanks to my interaction with Christian history, I can find a counternarrative to my culture, a story that pushes me toward the kingdom values of God where I surrender my plans and possessions for the work of God.

HOW TO USE CHRISTIAN TRADITION

In addition to providing a different perspective for our theology, Christian tradition helps us weigh the value of doctrines as we find their traces among Christians before us. If we discover a doctrine threaded throughout Christian tradition, then we can safely presume that we should take it seriously. On the other hand, we might read about doctrines previously held by the church and find that they represent only their times and have no bearing on us. For example, the doctrine of purgatory really caught on in the Middle Ages and was based on shaky biblical foundations.[14] The sale of indulgences to redeem souls from purgatory oppressed peasants, robbing them of their hard-earned money for the supposed relief of their suffering relatives. Mistakes and abuses like these throughout church history warn us, bidding that we form our theology carefully in context, otherwise we'll just as likely make similar grievous errors.

After praying and studying Scripture on a particular topic, every theologian should review the available church history and traditions as well. You can find a number of resources to learn more about Christian tradition both online and in bookstores. For well-known topics such as major doctrines and theologians, *Wikipedia* is a tremendous online resource for digging deeper into a particular issue. Even if an article isn't helpful, most entries have a long list of references and links to browse. In addition, a group of Christians have put together *Theopedia*, an online encyclopedia that focuses solely on Christian topics, although the quality of some articles is questionable. The websites www.mannacabana.com and www.zoecarnate .com are excellent places to find Christian resources such as creeds and documents from church history. In addition, simply searching for a particular item such as "Christian creeds" will produce more than enough options for a theologian to use. In a matter of seconds I found www.creeds.net, which lists just about every creed and confession from the 2000-year history of the church.

At a time when historical narrative has reached a sort of golden age, you can find many Christian biographies and Christian history texts. One of the most widely used texts is *The Story of Christianity* (New York: HarperOne, 1984, 1985) by Justo Gonzalez, a theologian from Latin America who has made significant contributions to contextual theology, specifically a modern branch of theology known as liberation theology. Gonzalez receives high marks both for the quality of his material and his polished narrative flow—traits that ensure his text's place as a standard in seminaries and Christian colleges.

Another theology text I find immensely helpful is Roger Olson's *The Story of Christian Theology* (Downers Grove, IL: InterVarsity, 1999). Olson digs through the major theological debates faced by the church, which sometimes can lead to dull sections. But the simple fact that he can make so much heavy theological content *mostly* readable is an astounding feat. The sheer breadth of this work is incredible, and he provides an excellent analysis of contemporary theology that will help many Christians discover their theological roots. By way of critique, I should mention that Olson reveals his Arminian[15] stripes by downplaying the importance of John Calvin. Lastly, Bruce Shelley has written an accessible book, *Church History in Plain Language* (Nashville: Thomas Nelson, 1996), which is popular among students.

Of course, forming theology in the postmodern context reveals one major weakness of many theology books and Christian theology in general: White male scholars primarily from Europe and the Mediterranean region dominate these collections. We have little in our historical archives from women and minority voices. Further, we can easily neglect the contributions of Eastern Orthodox Christians when we look into Christian tradition. And we should also remember that victors usually write the history, so even the most well-meaning historical accounts will lack some diversity that characterizes the historic church. To a certain extent we can hope to remedy these wrongs by listening to a greater collection of voices in the present, so that one group doesn't speak for all.

These books and articles help us connect with who we are, show us where our beliefs come from, demonstrate how reliable they've been throughout history (or whether they're relatively new), and help us weigh the value of our interpretations today. As we read Scripture and form theology in today's context, we should be wary of new doctrines that depart from the guiding consensus of Christians before us, especially the Apostles' and Nicene Creeds, which provide succinct summaries of our faith. Of course, Christians have never been perfect, but we should still pay careful notice to areas where Christians have consistently agreed throughout history. In addition, where Christians have made errors, we can learn lessons about the limits imposed by our context and remember that people one day might read what we've written and wonder how we could be so far off the mark.

We can begin putting our traditions to work by reading a book here and an article there, slowly accumulating an idea of our history that we can keep in mind while reading and interpreting Scripture. Even knowing a few prayers, creeds, or confessions will go a long way toward grounding us among the most essential doctrines affirmed by past Christians. We might not run every reading of Scripture past historic interpretation. That would be next to impossible. But we can familiarize ourselves with these doctrines that have been passed on to us, hold on to them, and then use them as a litmus test when we study Scripture and find a need to broaden our perspective.

I trust that even as we read up on our history, we'll be pleasantly surprised by what we find. I also hope that we'll learn to read

Scripture differently as a result. Contextual theology will take us to new places as we meet new challenges, but keep in mind that the brilliance of a new doctrine can quickly fade when compared to the glow of the carefully polished gems of our traditions.

▶ ▶ ▶ FOR FURTHER READING

- *Light from the Christian East: An Introduction to the Orthodox Tradition* (Downers Grove, IL: InterVarsity, 2007), by James R. Payton Jr.
- *Early Christian Doctrines* (New York: Continuum International, 2000), by J. N. D. Kelly
- *A Dictionary of Early Christian Biography: A Reference Guide to Over 800 Men and Women, Heretics, and Sects of the First Six Centuries* (Peabody, MA: Hendrickson, 1999), edited by Henry Wace and William C. Piercy
- *Historical Theology: An Introduction to the History of Christian Thought* (Malden, MA: Wiley-Blackwell, 1998), by Alister McGrath
- *The Christian Theology Reader* (Malden, MA: Wiley-Blackwell, 2006), by Alister McGrath
- *The Story of Christianity* (New York: HarperOne, 1984, 1985), by Justo Gonzalez
- *The Story of Christian Theology: Twenty Centuries of Tradition and Reform* (Downers Grove, IL: InterVarsity, 1999), by Roger E. Olson
- *The Mosaic of Christian Beliefs: Twenty Centuries of Unity & Diversity* (Downers Grove, IL: InterVarsity, 2002), by Roger E. Olson
- *A Concise History of Christian Doctrine* (Nashville: Abingdon, 2006), by Justo Gonzalez

- *A History of Christianity* (New York: HarperOne, 1975), by Kenneth Scott Latourette
- *Church History in Plain English* (Nashville: Thomas Nelson, 1996), by Bruce Shelley
- *Turning Points: Decisive Moments in the History of Christianity* (Grand Rapids, MI: Baker, 2001), by Mark Noll
- *A History of Christianity in the United States and Canada* (Grand Rapids, MI: Eerdmans, 1992), by Mark Noll
- *A Religious History of the American People* (New Haven, CT: Yale University Press, 1972), by Sydney Ahlstrom

For additional resources and discussion, see http://inamirrordimly .com/coffeehouse-theology/chapter-9.

A Web of Theology

This web illustrates the interconnected nature of Christian theology's sources and contexts.

Current chapter topic will be in bold.

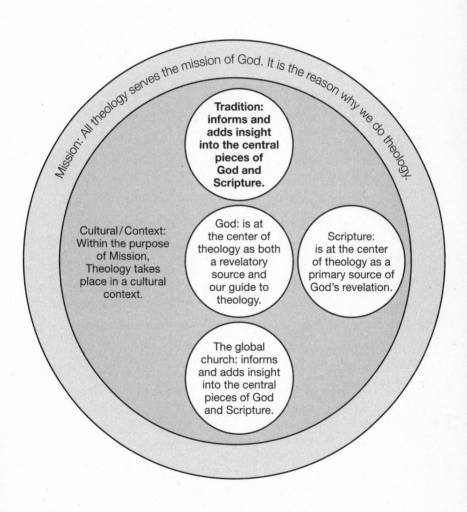

Mission: All theology serves the mission of God. It is the reason why we do theology.

Tradition: informs and adds insight into the central pieces of God and Scripture.

Cultural/Context: Within the purpose of Mission, Theology takes place in a cultural context.

God: is at the center of theology as both a revelatory source and our guide to theology.

Scripture: is at the center of theology as a primary source of God's revelation.

The global church: informs and adds insight into the central pieces of God and Scripture.

Chapter 10

THE GLOBAL CHURCH

Keeping Us Informed

The music carried over the homes and limestone streets of Jerusalem's old city. On virtually empty streets, melodies filled the void created by the absence of tourists and competing shopkeepers. I continued with my group of friends toward the music flowing from a predominantly Palestinian church in the Christian quarter, where we planned to attend a Sunday morning service.

The service felt like any evangelical meeting in North America. We began with prayer and then worship leaders fired up the overhead projector, slapped down transparencies, and started strumming the guitars. We didn't catch on too well during the singing, but did a touch better during the message because all non-Arabic speakers huddled into a separate room for a translation of the sermon. With a closed circuit television showing the preacher in the other room, a translator filled us in on the lesson.

I'm sure the sermon was excellent, but the offering time stood out for me. I clearly remember that someone talked about the difficulties of the Christians in Jericho—perhaps I couldn't shake this and completely missed the sermon as a result. This church wanted to deliver food and money to their fellow Christians in Jericho, but the Israeli checkpoints were almost impassible during the current intifada,[1] the Al-Aqsa Intifada that began in 2000. After taking the offering, they prayed for their brothers and sisters who were virtually walled off from them.

I simply never imagined that Christians in Jericho were suffering during the Israeli crack-down, not to mention the tensions they must face as religious outsiders amidst the more extreme elements on the Palestinian side. As a Christian in America, it's hard to imagine being in a religious minority, let alone being in such a volatile region.

But that's not all I thought about.

At that point in my life, as an American Christian, I described myself as generally pro-Israel. I didn't really understand the Palestinians or other Arabs, for that matter. The Arabs supposedly started a war in 1948,[2] the Israelis won, and, by the way, God seems to have this thing for the Jewish people. In my thinking prior to visiting Israel and the Palestinian territory, Israel's victory in the War for Independence plus the Jews' status as God's chosen people equaled little sympathy for the Palestinian cause. Besides, I believed God had a plan for Israel that didn't include a large Muslim population camped out on the temple mount.

I say all of this to my shame. At that point in my life, I viewed the Palestinians as more of a roadblock to God's plan than as individuals whom God loves as much as he loves me.

Without digging into the intricacies of Israeli settlers, Zionism, and the complex Palestinian/Arab situation, I'll just say the Palestinian Christians opened my eyes to some grievous oversights. These people were Christians, also the chosen people of God, and I'd ignored them.

This discovery sent my notion of the end times reeling and opened my eyes to the plan of God for the salvation of people of all nations, including the Palestinians, who have suffered through war, corrupt leadership, and deprivations most of us would find intolerable. In the course of a few hours, God's desire to save all people — even using the people of Israel as a light to *all nations* — took on a whole new meaning (see Isaiah 49:6).

My brief connection with a group of Palestinian Christians forever changed my confidence in relying on only my own perspective. Somehow I'd been reading the Bible in a way that marginalized an entire nation of people, something quite contrary to the plans of God. Rather than seeing the return of Christ as a reclamation of the Holy Land from Islam and the Arab peoples, I learned from the Palestinian Christians that God is working everywhere in the world, bringing redemption from the inside out among the hearts of these precious people.

If we want to enter into the essential work of understanding God in our everyday lives, we need to seek out Christians such as these Palestinians who might challenge us to completely rethink long-held assumptions or interpretations of Scripture that arise more from our cultural context than from the revelation of God. The only way to shake our limitations and to take steps toward a more complete understanding of the truth is to seek perspectives outside our own. Of course, we still look to God as the center of our theology and to Scripture as the primary source where God reveals himself. But just as we also consider the traditions and history of the church, we also gain great insights by seeking out the perspectives of global Christians to do contextual theology in the postmodern world, which values these diverse and multiple perspectives.

THE GLOBAL CHURCH AND POSTMODERNISM

"Back in India, my church will never divide over disagreements about theology."

You could have heard a pin drop in our theology class.

"Not even if your pastor teaches that Jesus isn't God or that the Bible is a myth?" asked one of my classmates.

"No, we never divide the church. If we need to discipline anyone, the elders just prevent those in error from tithing. That usually resolves things," said this student from India. He single-handedly took the steam out of our discussion about which doctrines are just cause for a church split.

Audible sighs — sighs of envy — came from the class filled with current and future pastors. Just imagine a church where Christians considered giving a privilege! No sermon series on giving, no year-end pleas to balance the budget. When it comes to finances, church in India sounded like a breeze. Of course, they still faced the matter of reconciling heresy and unity. I thought I had the right angle on this matter.

"What if your children — your young, impressionable children — are in a Sunday school class and the teachers of the class tell them that the Bible isn't true?" I asked. "Surely you wouldn't permit these people to stay in your church."

"I still wouldn't divide the church," countered the student from India. "Of course, I would confront the incorrect beliefs of the leaders."

Our professor joined in: "Good point. If we divide the church over a false teaching, who will guide the people in error back to the truth?"

In America, we regularly break off from people who are different from us. So it was shocking to find this level of commitment to unity even in the midst of heresy among Indian Christians. I know where our discussion would have gone that day without the bold stand for unity by our Indian classmate. We would have listed certain occasions where church division is permissible. After all, roughly half the churches I've attended resulted from a split from another congregation over differences involving worship styles, how to raise children, and even how to present the gospel message.

Since that discussion with my Christian classmate from India, I've never looked at doctrinal differences in quite the same light.

In order for Christian theology to thrive in the postmodern age, we desperately need to interact with Christians all across the world. Only then can we learn from the rich traditions and denominations that have grown up in various locations. If we've learned anything of value about the postmodern era, it's the benefit of diversity. And Christian theology only becomes stronger because of it.

Diversity in the postmodern context doesn't imply a simplistic, anything-goes relativism. Rather, diversity means an awareness of different perspectives that provide valuable insights. We can remain completely committed to certain beliefs, yet still learn from different perspectives. Even if our basic beliefs don't change, we might sharpen what we believe through dialogue with Christians outside our own context. By interacting with a diverse group of beliefs other than our own, we can constantly hone our views and add fresh dimensions that we could never have found on our own. In a complex world where we struggle to pin down truth and where language can be vague, our pursuit of the truth requires as many perspectives as we can find to fill in as many gaps as possible.

Whether we read a personal blog, an article, or a book that expresses the beliefs of Christians elsewhere in the world, we'll encounter Christians who see the world quite differently from us. They challenge our interpretations of Scripture by presenting fresh possibilities and angles we might be missing. This serves to sharpen our theology by leading to a broader understanding of God and his revealed truth.

LEARNING FROM THE GLOBAL CHURCH

On the evening of April 6, 1994, Rwandan President Juvénal Habyarimana and Cyprien Ntaryamira, the Hutu president of Burundi, perished when their plane was shot down. Government and military leaders entered into tense negotiations as radical Hutus prepared to carry out their plan for wiping out Tutsis and conservative Hutus.[3] On the following day, conservative members of the Rwandan government were either assassinated or chased out of the country. To the shock of the global community, the radical Hutus carried out a well-organized genocide that left roughly 800,000 people dead. We should take note that Rwanda is generally known as a Christian nation.

Unfortunately, Christians in Rwanda didn't always work against the dark forces sweeping through the land. Instead, they had a history of enforcing the cultural barriers between Hutus and Tutsis, and on a few occasions went so far as assisting in the murders.[4] According to a story in the *Washington Post*, "Human rights groups have documented several incidents in which Christian clerics allowed Tutsis to seek refuge in churches, then surrendered them to Hutu death squads, as well as instances of Hutu priests and ministers encouraging their congregations to kill Tutsis."[5] Even if these kinds of incidents were limited, the cultural captivity of some Rwandan Christians to the values of their context rather than the values of God's kingdom is worth noting. Instead of challenging the country's accepted ethnic divisions with the apostle Paul's words in Galatians 3:28 ("there is neither Jew nor Greek . . . in Christ Jesus"), some Christians in

Rwanda abandoned the healing message of the gospel.

Of course, Christians in *every* nation have their blind spots, so no one church will ever embody a completely pure version of Christianity. In fact, while theology should always be a locally grown undertaking, it will suffer from a limited perspective and lead to errors if we don't cross-fertilize our local theology with voices from the global church.

Missions

When we look to the global church for insight into theology, we'll often see Scripture in an entirely new light. For example, American theologian Scot McKnight shares about Mark Powell's book *What Do They Hear?* where American, Russian, and Tanzanian students share their readings of the prodigal son parable.[6] Curiously, the vast majority of Americans focused on the son's misuse of money, while missing the part about the famine. On the other hand, Russian students overwhelmingly noted the importance of the famine, while Tanzanian students saw the mistreatment of the son, an immigrant, among the foreign farmers. Americans often zip right past the prodigal's desire for pig slop or his dealings with his employers and focus on his sprint back to the father for an emotional reunion so they can talk about grace and forgiveness. It makes me wonder what elements of this story I've been missing.

Beyond these "Aha!" moments that provide a new insight into Scripture, Christians from other parts of the world can significantly challenge our beliefs and how we interpret the Bible. Learning about the experiences of Marilyn Lazslo, an American missionary to Papua New Guinea, revolutionized my own theological growth during my college years. As I heard her stories at a mission conference and read her book *Mission Possible* (Carol Stream, IL: Tyndale, 1998), I found myself questioning the prohibition on women in church leadership advocated by my church and other Christians.

Marilyn knew from a young age that she wanted to be a missionary. Yet only after she secured a comfortable teaching job did she sense God prompting her to follow that desire. After receiving her training in Bible translation from Wycliffe, she departed her native Indiana and traveled to Papua New Guinea, just off the coast of Australia. While she sometimes worked with her sister, often Marilyn was the only missionary in Hauna village, home of the Sepik Iwam people. She served as the clinician, school teacher, Bible teacher, and much more in this remote jungle village. Starting from scratch, she created a written alphabet for the Sepik Iwam with the help of some young boys and the village elders. She used these raw materials not only to teach the people how to read, but also to teach them the Bible, which she worked hard to translate into their native language.

Perhaps we hear so many stories about missionaries that we gloss over the details. But hearing about Marilyn raised an important point: She taught the Bible to people. If she traveled back to America, some churches would not only prohibit her from preaching on Sunday morning, they would also stop her from teaching men in Sunday school — although a slideshow about her work might pass.

If a woman wants to teach the Bible to men, some Christians would object on the basis of 1 Corinthians 14:33-35 and 1 Timothy 2:12. The first passage commands women to be silent when gathered in the congregation, while the second passage simply forbids women from teaching. While a wide range of disagreement exists about these passages,[7] as for me, I was surprised to read how God used Marilyn to grow a church among the Sepik Iwam people. I shared earlier how Christian friends and family members changed my views on this issue. But long before I read that there is neither male nor female in Christ, I was presented with the quandary of Marilyn Lazslo. Throughout her story, she never mentioned any qualms about these passages, nor did any of the natives express any concerns. I'd always believed that women weren't allowed to teach in church, just as my church had always instructed. But with the introduction of this Christian woman's work on the other side of the world, my theology hit a jolting speed bump. While I was against women speaking in American churches, I saw no contradiction in supporting a woman — the only missionary to the tribe — who was clearly teaching men the Bible.

How could I approve of one action on the other side of the world, yet condemn it in my own backyard? This question gnawed at me, challenging my beliefs about women in ministry and forcing a look at the darker side of my theology. Specifically, I had to face whether or not I believed a woman could teach the Bible to a race of people without the same education as I but not be capable of teaching educated white people like me. The racial overtones are hard to ignore, and, as I continued to struggle with this doctrine over the years, I ended up believing that it's all-or-nothing: Either women can't teach the Bible to men in *every* setting, or Paul's instructions concerning women in church gatherings applied only to a specific situation with his readers. However you slice it, both interpretations have holes and inconsistencies. But the work of God around the world provided an added push in my theology toward permitting women to teach men.

This situation illustrates American theologian Ray Anderson's desire to open our theologies to "those who have stories to tell of God's power and presence and, who themselves, have been transformed, healed, and empowered by the reality of Christ."[8] Because of Marilyn's powerful ministry in Papua New Guinea, I began leaning toward permitting women to teach in church gatherings. And if these passages in 1 Corinthians and 1 Timothy couldn't be interpreted in a strictly literal sense, I began to wonder if others existed. One missionary on the other side of the world forever changed my theology in significant ways.

We could add many other perspectives, experiences, and beliefs from the global church to Marilyn's. As we read Scripture in our local context and arrive at some conclusions about its meaning, our work isn't done. We then open our interpretations to the insights from our traditions and from Christians all over the world. These other voices might change our beliefs, we might agree to disagree, or perhaps we affirm one another.

Learning from the global church is a gradual process that we integrate into our everyday lives and that we can actively participate in because Christians around the world need to hear our unique perspectives as well. We can read blogs and books by Christians in other contexts in order to better evaluate our own interpretations of Scripture and the beliefs we run into every day. In fact, I recently read about a Bible study program on TV that promised to show people how to live successfully—a promise vastly different from the liberation theology of Latin America that I've read about in several books. With this knowledge of another perspective in mind, I'm better equipped to evaluate the prosperity gospel that makes the rounds among some Christians in America.

Global Theologians

Beyond the individual stories from the global church that inform theology, we sometimes discover theological perspectives unique to particular regions. While the western church has exported its theological tradition all over the world, local theologians throughout the world give voice to the specific theological angles of their homelands.

Latin America's theological emphasis on liberation theology might be one of the most well-known. Though American theologians should never adopt another region's theology in whole, Latin America's theology provides a helpful critique of America's prosperity gospel and our concepts of blessing and stewardship. Latin Americans typically face difficult economic circumstances, if not outright oppression. When they read the Bible, they see God taking the side of the poor, promising to bring relief and eventual deliverance. So they closely tie the gospel with social justice. Theologians in this context struggle to avoid tying themselves too closely to the revolutionary movements sweeping through their regions but rather live as revolutionary Christians in their day-to-day lives. Justo Gonzalez speaks of sacramental service not revolutionary action as the means of breaking exploitation.[9]

While liberation theology has its own problems, as Americans, we can still value the alternate perspective it provides. Americans are tempted to read the Bible under the assumption that God takes our side and caters to our needs—I mean, who wouldn't? When Paul says, "And my God will meet all your needs according to his glorious riches in Christ Jesus" (Philippians 4:19), I know I find it tempting to read this as a guarantee that God will take care of my finances, employment, and other physical needs. If I'm truly a child of God, shouldn't I expect my heavenly Father to take care of all my needs? However, I can hardly imagine what a person living in poverty thinks of these verses, and that's why I need to dialogue with the interpretations of global theologians.

Neither Americans nor Latin Americans have God completely figured out, but as an American, I appreciate the corrective provided by these theologians south of the border to the narrative of the American Dream that threatens to taint the theology in my own nation. I'm certain that at other times, Americans provide some much-needed perspective to Latin American theologians as well. Neither wealth nor poverty exclusively signify or guarantee blessing, so we can only find the truth as we carry on a robust dialogue among the theologies of various cultures. We only make our theologies stronger through this connection of theologians faithfully thinking about God in their local contexts.[10]

This again points to the importance of comparing our understanding of Scripture with the perspectives of Christians around the world. As an American, I simply can't see every angle of the truth. So I continue to read about the beliefs of Christians around the world to gain additional insights and contribute my own observations to the discussion. Learning the diverse views of global Christians helps me reread the Bible with fresh eyes, leading to interpretations that reflect a fuller representation of God's revelation. A dialogue with global Christians provides an ongoing cycle that consistently sends us back to the Scriptures to find more of God's revelation from new perspectives.

FORMING THEOLOGY IN THE LOCAL CHURCH

By including the global church's ministers, theologians, and lay leaders with our sources for theology, we'll be better prepared to form contextual theology that takes into account the various perspectives on God throughout the world. Our broad sweep through the global church ends with the church in our own local context. In this community, we embody and live out the truth of our theologies. Theologian Robert Webber said, "Truth is not proven, it is embodied by individuals and by the community known as the church."[11] As we read Scripture in gatherings with friends, in Sunday school classes, in small groups, and during Sunday morning services, our goal isn't forming a theology that we can use to judge whether or not someone can join us. Instead, we seek to know God so that we can embody him in our world.[12] The local church helps us in this process and keeps us on track.

We need the global voices of the church because our own

theological partners will most likely share our same affinities and blind spots. Yet these local contributors to our theological reflections are every bit as crucial. These friends and teachers will provide accountability and guidance as we seek to form and live theology. These people will guard us from slipping into heresy or adopting doctrines contrary to the gospel.

Our Christian communities are immersed in a context, and we must work out our beliefs on theological issues as they come up. Theology serves as the church's tool while we live as Christ's ambassadors, the representatives of his kingdom in a foreign land. As we live out the truth of the gospel in a local context, we'll always benefit by interacting with the global voices of the church.

God's mission encompasses the entire world, and we should never approach this calling as if we can do it on our own. As God's kingdom advances, we need a practical, well-thought-out theology if we desire to join him on his mission.

▶ ▶ ▶ FOR FURTHER READING

- *Africa Bible Commentary: A One-Volume Commentary Written by 70 African Scholars* (Grand Rapids, MI: Zondervan, 2006), edited by Tokunboh Adeyemo
- *Manana: Christian Theology from a Hispanic Perspective* (Nashville: Abingdon, 1990), by Justo Gonzalez
- *Santa Biblia: The Bible Through Hispanic Eyes* (Nashville: Abingdon, 1996), by Justo Gonzalez
- *InterVarsity Press Women's Bible Commentary* (Downers Grove, IL: InterVarsity, 2002), edited by Catherine Clark Kroeger and Mary J. Evans
- *Learning About Theology from the Third World* (Grand Rapids, MI: Zondervan, 1990), by William A. Dyrness

- *Emerging Voices in Global Christian Theology* (Wipf & Stock, 2003), by William A. Dyrness
- *Wisdom of Daughters* (Philadelphia: Innisfree, 2001), edited by Reta Halteman Finger and Kari Sandhaas
- *Exclusion and Embrace: A Theological Exploration of Identity, Otherness, and Reconciliation* (Nashville: Abingdon, 1996), by Miroslav Volf
- *Return to Babel: Global Perspectives on the Bible* (Louisville, KY: Westminster John Knox, 1999), edited by John R. Levison and Priscilla Pope-Levison
- *Introducing Asian American Theologies* (Maryknoll, NY: Orbis, 2008), by Jonathan Tan
- *Faithful Generations: Race and New Asian American Churches* (Piscataway, NJ: Rutgers University Press, 2005), by Russell Jeung
- *The Heavenly Man: The Remarkable True Story of Chinese Christian Brother Yun* (London: Monarch, 2002), by Brother Yun and Paul Hattaway

For additional resources and discussion, see http://inamirrordimly .com/coffeehouse-theology/chapter-10.

A Web of Theology

This web illustrates the interconnected nature of Christian theology's sources and contexts.

Current chapter topic will be in bold.

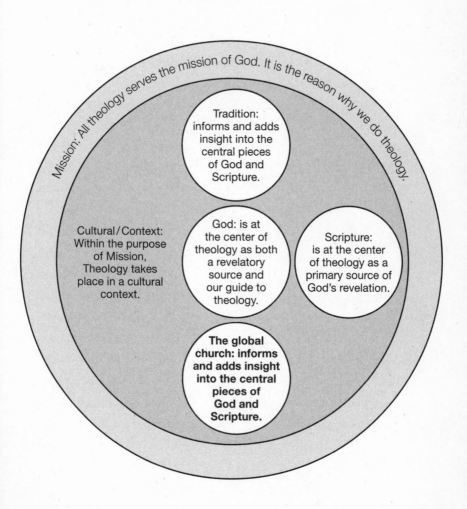

Mission: All theology serves the mission of God. It is the reason why we do theology.

Tradition: informs and adds insight into the central pieces of God and Scripture.

Cultural / Context: Within the purpose of Mission, Theology takes place in a cultural context.

God: is at the center of theology as both a revelatory source and our guide to theology.

Scripture: is at the center of theology as a primary source of God's revelation.

The global church: informs and adds insight into the central pieces of God and Scripture.

Chapter 11

OUR LOVE OF GOD
UNITES US IN THEOLOGY

My parents separated when I was just a year old, so I've never known a time when my parents were married. Divorce puts a lot of strain on families, and it took years to iron out all of the details. Still, we all made it through those tough times of sharing holidays and the childhood nightmare that naturally comes with joint custody, constantly tearing yourself from one family to be with another and then repeating the cycle—although I hasten to add this was the best way to arrange things out of the options available. While my parents and their respective families fought their share of battles, I never doubted their love for me.

My mom and dad both ended up in happy new marriages, and I keep in touch with all parties. One final hurdle for my parents in relation to me came on my wedding day. My mom and dad hadn't been at an event together for years, so I experienced a bit of tension, not to mention worried about how the extended families would gel during the reception. Some probably hadn't seen each other since my parents' wedding.

With the guests all seated, our ceremony began. I promptly sobbed through the whole thing, a dove flew overhead, and we snapped tons of pictures all without incident. At the reception, Julie's cousins struck up a set of classic rock, and the crowd began dancing. Then a miracle of sorts happened. My father has two daughters from his remarriage, while my mom has one daughter. My mother's daughter ran over to my father's youngest daughter and dragged her onto the dance floor—they had the time of their lives! In fact, everyone had a wonderful time at our wedding, as family members who sometimes sat on opposite sides of family court chatted over drinks.

Seeing my step-sisters dancing symbolized the most amazing part of our wedding: regardless of harsh words, hurt feelings, or bitterness, all of my family could unite in their love for Julie and me. Our wedding showed how two families—who couldn't be more opposite or divided—can come together because of their common love. My family still talks about this life-changing day at family gatherings.

ANOTHER GATHERING OF LOVE

When I think about the church, I realize we have so much in common when we talk about our love for Jesus, the presence of the Holy Spirit, and the love of the Father for his children. Even if our Christian family has splintered and shattered over time, we can gather around God the Father, Jesus the Son, and the Holy Spirit, I'm content to say we have enough in common. When we celebrate the work of Jesus and the coming of God's kingdom, the divisions brought by denominations melt away under our one Lord. Sure, our theological traditions and heritage have wonderful value. Yet I can't help thinking that heaven won't have different sections for different denominations like some cosmic political convention, with placards indicating where Catholics, Baptists, Episcopalians, Lutherans, and so on should seat their delegations. So why *overemphasize* the importance of these distinctions now? We have one Lord, one faith, and one baptism — even if denominations can't agree on some of the particulars.

Doing theology in the postmodern context challenges us to read Scripture with an awareness of how our culture influences who we are and how we see the world, while dialoguing with Christians from history and around the world. This process involves reading Scripture, and then rereading Scripture in light of what our traditions and global believers teach us. While it sounds like a formula, contextual theology really only involves a commitment to reading Scripture while learning from Christians who have different perspectives.

Of course, we'll likely have disagreements with Christians within our own denominations, and who knows what conflicts will flare up when we dialogue with Christians who hold beliefs different from ours. Contextual theology has the potential to become pretty messy when we run into doctrines that unsettle beliefs we consider important. Other Christians might possess a broader understanding of salvation, a greater reverence for tradition, or a higher regard for the gifts of the Spirit. How can we learn from these believers and at the same time prevent further divisions?

The answer lies in what all Christians have in common: a love for God. Our love for God can motivate us toward understanding God through our study of Scripture. Jesus said the greatest command is to love God, followed closely by loving our neighbors. So our love for God needs to supply the framework for any study of God. If we truly want to understand how God reveals himself in Scripture, we'll miss the point unless love drives our theology. The apostle Paul wrote:

I pray that out of his glorious riches he may strengthen
you with power through his Spirit in your inner being, so
that Christ may dwell in your hearts through faith. And
I pray that you, being rooted and established in love, may
have power, together with all the saints, to grasp how wide
and long and high and deep is the love of Christ, and to
know this love that surpasses knowledge—that you may be
filled to the measure of all the fullness of God. (Ephesians
3:16-19)

Far from fragmenting Christians over their differences, the
ongoing process of theology should draw diverse Christians together
under the common goal of understanding this God we love. Rather
than settling on our doctrines and setting out to defend them, the
value of different perspectives in the postmodern age should result in
a greater dependence on other Christians. We can unite even with
believers who hold vastly different doctrinal views because of our
love for our Lord.

THEOLOGY IS NEVER DONE

When I think of theology, I like to imagine an ongoing conversation
that not only takes place in the present among my friends, but also
across oceans and across the falling sands of time.

The excitement and challenge of theology lies in the way it refuses
to be done once and for all. New circumstances demand fresh readings of Scripture, and theologians will come to the best conclusions
possible in the current context. While wrestling with the biblical text
and prayerfully meditating on it, we can gain priceless perspectives
by consulting all available sources of Christian tradition and fellow
believers both from our hometowns and in other lands.

Again, we don't need to follow any particular formula to do contextual theology, as long as the Bible itself stands as the primary source in our studies, above any teaching from tradition or any doctrine advocated by other Christians in the global church. Contextual theology requires that we simply pay attention to our surrounding culture and then read and reread the Bible while also taking notice of our traditions and Christians from around the world. While the core beliefs at the center of our theology—at the center of our web of beliefs—might never change, we will always be open to change.

I'm glad that my theology has changed over time because, to be honest, I've been very wrong more than once. If I had to pick the biggest change in my theology that resulted from dialoguing with other Christians and reevaluating the way I read Scripture, it would have to be my views on the Holy Spirit.

At one time in my Christian life, I was skeptical of spiritual gifts such as tongues, being slain in the Spirit, and other manifestations of the Spirit. I remember listening to Hank Hanegraaff, the suave radio Bible Answer Man, decrying the Toronto Blessing that took place in 1997 at the Toronto Airport Vineyard Christian Fellowship. People were falling onto the floor and laughing, crying, or passing out completely.[1] They claimed to have had visions of swords, flames, and who knows what else. Hanegraaff declared that these people were clearly deviating from the teachings of Scripture and should cut out all of this flopping around on the floor.[2] I didn't know any other Christians who acted this way, so I just took Hank's word that the Toronto Blessing Christians were wrong. Sure, the Holy Spirit shows up in the Bible, but today is another matter. I always thought of the Holy Spirit as getting things started in the early church, and then stepping back into a more peripheral, behind-the-scenes support role.

Fast forward about five years. I met Julie, a Vermont girl, while studying in Jerusalem, and went home with her to meet her family in northern Vermont where they ministered in a prison. Besides the emotional scars from the constant teasing of one of her brothers, I vividly remember learning from her parents about their time up at the Toronto Blessing. Toronto wasn't just a neat conference where they took notes in a binder and afterward stacked it on a shelf. Toronto marked the turning point for them and their ministry. They looked back to that time as a deepening in their walks with the Lord and the infusion of the Holy Spirit into every facet of their prison ministry. A little surprised and unsure what to think, I went along with it, trusting that these nice and reasonable people probably weren't locked into some dangerous movement or heresy. They showed me a video about the revival at the Toronto Airport Vineyard. And while sobbing, laughing, and passing out—in church that is—were completely foreign to me, nothing about it seemed wrong.

During another visit to see Julie, I accompanied her parents into the prison for a church service. There I was, a conservative Baptist who had absolutely no grid for manifestations of the Holy Spirit. We sat down in a circle, began to pray, and then "crazy stuff"[3] started to happen. People prayed in all kinds of languages, men who received prayer became ridiculously hot and sweaty, and a few guys receiving intense prayer just dropped to the floor. Some expressed praise, others received physical healing, and still others received emotional healing for the scars left by troubled pasts. Nothing evil or unbiblical happened—just a lot of God's redemptive work.

My neat and tidy grid fell to pieces. The Holy Spirit has a powerful hold in this world, and I began to see that clearly in the prison with Julie's parents. After learning about the revival in Toronto and then learning from Christians who believe the Holy Spirit still shows up in concrete and powerful ways, I started to read Scripture differently, I prayed differently, and I approached just about every other part of my Christian walk differently.

Thankfully, my beliefs about the Holy Spirit weren't hardened to the point of rejecting the ministry of Julie's parents. I could have just stood up and left when the "crazy stuff" started to happen. Well, given that we were in a prison, I could have at least *tried* to leave. Still, I willingly stayed and learned and changed. I now read the Bible with a greater awareness of how the Holy Spirit works in our world, and consequently I pray with a new urgency and expectation that God desires to do something wonderful.

We all face the same challenge of holding to central beliefs while allowing room for Christians from history and around the world to add different perspectives to shape our beliefs in an ongoing dialogue. This process is never done. What's important in contextual theology is our willingness to dialogue, to learn, and to grow.

THEOLOGY BUILDS OUR DEPENDENCE ON OTHER CHRISTIANS

If we hold to the core beliefs of Christianity such as those expressed in the Nicene Creed, yet we boldly seek other Christians to provide fresh angles on our other interpretations of Scripture, we make ourselves dependent on other Christians. And that's a good thing.

Of course, this is a far cry from arguing with other Christians who disagree with us. Instead of arguing, we can use our disagreements to our advantage—seeking out why other Christians hold different beliefs and why they reject our perspectives. While this might not be easy to put into practice, as we face our own weaknesses and the strengths of others we gain tremendous opportunities for growth. We might not change our minds about any doctrinal issues. But if and when we do, it will be for very good reasons.

If I had to pick one group in Christianity whose theology I found hard to appreciate, it would have to be Roman Catholicism. I grew up as a Catholic and even endured the optimistic prediction of many that

I would become a priest one day. I knew that my desire to be married made becoming a priest rather difficult, but I smiled and nodded all the same. As a Catholic, I attended mass every week, confessed regularly, and progressed through the typical sacrament program. As a young teen, I started to read the Bible for myself—a sleek NIV thinline version. A priest, who was probably more concerned about the fundamentalist church I'd started attending than the Bible itself, cautioned me that reading the Bible for myself could be dangerous and that only priests should read and interpret the Bible.

Well, that did it! Once you tell a teenager not to do something, most have to try it. In my case, I wasn't a rebellious teenager trying cigarettes, drugs, or sex. Instead, I wanted to read the Bible without the Catholic Church peering over my shoulder. Maybe I saw myself as a mini–Martin Luther fighting "the system." I staged my own little reformation. As I read the Bible over the following years, I compiled a laundry list of problems with the Catholic Church—especially the absolution offered by the priest during confession, and what I took to be the blending of faith and works.

I eventually started attending an evangelical Baptist church. Years passed, and I wholeheartedly embraced my evangelical church, cutting myself off from the traditions of the Catholic Church and its questionable doctrines. I attended a Christian college with precisely one Catholic student (at least that I knew of), a tall kid who ambled about campus with a huge wooden cross flopping about on his chest. I eyed him with suspicion, not sure how a Catholic could really have saving faith in Christ when works were mixed into the salvation plan.

And then in seminary one of my theology professors—a Baptist to boot—blew me away in his theology class. He spent an entire day talking about the wisdom of the Catholic view of sacraments and explaining how Roman Catholics don't really believe good works earn someone's way into heaven.[4] At another point in the semester, we also discussed the Catholic view of tradition that sees Scripture and tradition as inseparably linked.

The whole idea of learning from Roman Catholicism was a new one for me. Up to that point, I was more interested in debunking Catholic beliefs. Still, this class opened my eyes to the valuable contributions of Catholic theology to the mosaic[5] of Christian beliefs. I could list several, but the most important lesson involved the importance of our traditions, and as I confronted the importance of our Christian history, I began to wonder what it would look like for evangelicals to dialogue with our traditions as we read Scripture.

Learning to appreciate my Catholic brothers and sisters in Christ was a major part of my Christian growth. I went from resenting this branch of the faith to truly appreciating its unique contributions. When we learn from Christians we disagree with, we stretch our theology and find out which parts are strong and which are weak. Just as I learned to appreciate the value of understanding Christian history by reading about the Catholic views of tradition, we stand to gain much by seeking out the views of Christians from a diversity of backgrounds. As we discuss, read, and learn, we find ourselves looking at Scripture from fresh perspectives and sometimes forming slightly revised interpretations.

THEOLOGY DRAWS US CLOSER TO GOD

Theology is open to the entire family of God. Because theology is the ongoing process of understanding the God we love, we need one another. Far from dividing Christians, theology draws us together as we seek to understand our Lord and Savior. These might seem like high ideals for a religion marked by divisions, splits, and excommunications throughout the years. Still, as we look at God through a postmodern lens that finds truth through a variety of perspectives, we have an opportunity to acknowledge our common goal of understanding God. We learn about theology because we love God, and we love one another because we love the same God and seek to know him more perfectly.

If love for God and for one another guides us while we form theology, then we will be wary of accumulating knowledge as a matter of pride. Sometimes theology debates are little more than contests to show off who knows more. Instead of working toward the truth as a community by dialoguing with a variety of perspectives, these theological contests become fights to the end, where only one point of view survives—a theological cage match if you will. In the midst of a divisive theological debate within the Corinthian church, the apostle Paul made an interesting statement: "Now about food sacrificed to idols: We know that we all possess knowledge. Knowledge puffs up, but love builds up. The man who thinks he knows something does not yet know as he ought to know. But the man who loves God is known by God" (1 Corinthians 8:1-3). I don't think that Paul intended to say anything against knowledge. Instead, he offered a corrective to the church, reminding us that all pursuit of knowledge should be motivated by love—a love that seeks the best for God and the people of God.

Paul essentially said, "Big deal—we all know something." Knowledge is fine, but it doesn't build up the church in the same way love does. In fact, knowledge has a tendency to make puffy people think more of themselves than warranted. The main thing worth knowing is how to love God and to build people up through love.

Theology isn't about constructing an arsenal of knowledge that we use to shoot down the beliefs of our "opponents." Theology is about loving God and one another more perfectly. When we toss aside our squabbles in order to join fellow builders, we'll discover how theology motivated by love will build a stronger Christian community and deepen our love for the God we're learning about. At the end of the day, all Christians can agree that we are committed to loving God through theology and joining the cause of God's kingdom. My earnest prayer is that everyone seeking to understand God in today's culture will accept this invitation and challenge to participate in reflecting on God in everyday life.

FINDING NEW WAYS TO LOVE GOD

We began our study of contextual theology with a question, "Where do our beliefs about God come from?" While our culture is a lens that we peer through, we form our beliefs about God by studying Scripture under the guidance of the Holy Spirit and then examine our conclusions by dialoguing with Christians from the past and from around the world. This theology helps us speak with relevance in our postmodern age. We face the challenge of putting to use a spectrum of perspectives in our complex world while living in the revealed truth of God in a world where the truth is sometimes hard to come by.

Thankfully, Christians rely on the revelation of God through the Holy Spirit, Scripture, and the Christian church to lead us into the truth. We seek to understand our culture so that we can overcome our blind spots and any elements of our culture that run counter to the values of God in order to avoid mixing our culture's values into our interpretations of Scripture. We also listen to Christians in other times and cultures who read the Bible through their own local lens, realizing that we need the insights of one another to reach beyond our own observations.

So contextual theology ends up being an ongoing process, a conversation we have between the Bible and the influences of our culture, traditions, and global Christians. We use this kind of theology to reach a more complete understanding of God, and our love for God drives us to continue working on knowing him better.

When we read, study, and discuss what other Christians have to say, we take our first steps onto the dance floor. We might not know our partners very well, and we might even harbor some suspicions about them. Perhaps you don't agree with many of the beliefs you find in the traditions and global theology of Christianity. Just remember, our goal isn't agreeing on every point, but rather better understanding the God we all love. From that perspective, we can dance with these partners because we share a common love, even if we express and understand that love in very different ways.

In spite of our past failures, our present mistakes, and our future mishaps, let's boldly step out onto the dance floor and take part in the celebration of our God. Each of our partners knows a different aspect of God, experiences God in a unique way, and loves God for a different reason. We'd be crazy to pass up this opportunity to see God from a whole new angle, to plumb new depths into the mystery of God, or to find new ways to love our Lord.

NOTES

CHAPTER 2

1. Ann Lamott, *Bird by Bird* (New York: Anchor, 1994), 22.
2. See comments under the following blog post: http://inamirrordimly.com/2007/02/12/young-earth-creationist-studies-fossils-from-65-million-years-ago/.
3. Biblical Theological Seminary provides an excellent response to Dan Brown's book at http://www.biblical.edu/pages/connect/da-vinci-code.htm (Accessed March 17, 2008).
4. Not counting the shelves of Christian spirituality books, I'm in the ballpark of 200+ theology books. Just in case you were wondering.
5. DeBorst, Ruth Padilla, "Liberate My People," *Christianity Today*, August 2007, http://www.christianvisionproject.com/2007/08/liberate_my_people.html. (Accessed Nov. 18, 2007).

CHAPTER 3

1. *Cambridge Dictionaries Online*, s.v. "Culture," http://dictionary .cambridge.org/define.asp?key=18888&dict=CALD.

2. My characterization here of dualism is very simplistic. For a more complete treatment, see George Eldon Ladd, *A Theology of the New Testament* (Grand Rapids, MI: Eerdmans, 1993), 268–272.

3. Asian American churches come in a wide variety. I'm sure that different Asian American churches define respect in different ways. But the point of the conversation with my friend centered around the generally different standards for respect between the two cultures.

4. Not to mention the printing press that made owning a Bible a real possibility.

5. The worst of these religious wars was the Thirty Years War (1618–1648), although we should also note that Protestants spent a great deal of time killing one another in Europe after the Reformation in the 1500s.

6. For some valuable thoughts on this perspective, see Frederica Matthewes-Green in *The Church in Emerging Culture: Five Perspectives*, ed. Leonard Sweet (Grand Rapids, MI: Zondervan, 2003), 178–179.

7. Lesslie Newbigin, *The Gospel in a Pluralist Society* (Grand Rapids, MI: Eerdmans, 1989), 220.

CHAPTER 4

1. See *The Luminous Dusk: Finding God in the Deep, Still Places* (Grand Rapids, MI: Eerdmans, 2006), by Dale C. Allison for more about the changes of modern society and their effects on how we experience God.

2. Justo Gonzalez, *The Story of Christianity* (Peabody, MA: Prince Press, 2007), 133.

3. Daniel J. Boorstin, *The Discoverers: A History of Man's Search to Know His World and Himself* (New York: Vintage Books, 1985), 322–323.

4. Boorstin, 325–326.

5. Diarmaid MacCulloch, *The Reformation: A History* (New York: Penguin, 2005), 685–688.

6. Trevor Hart, *Faith Thinking: The Dynamics of Christian Theology* (Downers Grove, IL: InterVarsity, 1995), 31.

7. Robert Greer, *Mapping Postmodernism* (Downers Grove, IL: InterVarsity, 2003), 30.

8. Merold Westphal, *Overcoming Ontotheology* (New York: Fordham University Press, 2001), 81.

9. Gonzalez, 122–123.

10. Nancey Murphy, *Beyond Liberalism and Fundamentalism* (Harrisburg, PA: Trinity Press International, 1996), 12.

11. Stanley Grenz, *A Primer on Postmodernism* (Grand Rapids: Eerdmans, 1996), 62.

12. Grenz, 67–71.

13. I am indebted to Nancey Murphy's book *Beyond Liberalism and Fundamentalism: How Modern and Postmodern Philosophy Set the Theological Agenda* (Harrisburg, PA: Trinity Press International, 1996) for these categories. Guidance was also provided by Dr. John Franke.

14. For more on modernism see *The Cambridge Introduction to Modernism* (New York: Cambridge University Press, 2007) or *The Oxford Companion to Philosophy* (New York: Oxford University Press, 2005).

15. Greer, 25.

16. Steven Best and Douglas Kellner, *The Postmodern Adventure* (New York: Guilford Press, 2001), 109.

CHAPTER 5

1. For a different take on postmodernism, see *Above All Earthly Pow'rs: Christ in a Postmodern World* (Grand Rapids, MI: Eerdmans, 2006), by David Wells.

2. The research of George Barna reveals that among the young adult "Mosaic" generation—those born between 1984 and 2002—32 percent are committed to the Christian faith, while 33 percent attend church. This is a drop compared to 54 percent and 49 percent respectively for the elders and baby boomers (Barna Group, "Church Attendance," http://www .barna.org/FlexPage.aspx?Page=Topic&TopicID=10). Accessed March 17, 2008).

3. Though there are exceptions, for the most part the Western world has shifted from a modern age in history (roughly 1500 to 1970) to a postmodern age (1970 to today). *Postmodernism* technically entered into our language in the 1920s through architecture, although it wasn't until the 1970s that postmodern philosophy gained a strong following in universities, especially in linguistics and literature. Various opinions abound regarding the status of postmodernism, and whether this is the best word to describe our times. Whatever we call the changes in our world—and it changed significantly between 1900 and 2000—a new philosophy drives the world that we'll call postmodernism, even if some have justifiably tired of the term. In my opinion, *postmodernism* is the most likely name for this shift and its aftershocks in our popular culture, because this term captures the revolutionary spirit of the new age against the modern world (in the sense that "post"

refers to something after modernism).

4. Philosopher and theologian Stanley Grenz favored a comparison between the top-down leadership of the original *Star Trek* and the communal-consensus leadership found in *Star Trek: The Next Generation*. We can also see the same trends when we stack the traditional Sherlock Holmes, who solved crimes with his astute observation and reason, beside the team-centered approach of investigators in the TV drama *CSI*.

5. One of the most fertile places for the development of postmodernism was France. However, since this work is presenting an American perspective and reaction, I won't be able to deal with the global manifestations of postmodernism.

6. Brian McLaren, "An Open Letter to Chuck Colson," http://www.brianmclaren.net/archives/000269.html.

7. For further discussion about the traits of postmodernism, see Stanley Grenz's *A Primer on Postmodernism* (Grand Rapids: Eerdmans, 1996), 7–8.

8. Relying on witnesses seemed crucial in the book of Acts. See 1:8; 2:32; 3:15; 5:32; 10:39; 10:41; 13:31.

9. Nancey Murphy, *Beyond Liberalism and Fundamentalism* (Harrisburg, PA: Trinity Press International, 1996), 105.

10. That's not to say that news anchors on prime-time programs aren't significant, only that they're part of a growing crowd. For better and for worse, their monopoly on the news has ended.

11. For more on this metaphor, see W. V. O. Quine, "Two Dogmas of Empiricism," in *From a Logical Point of View* (Cambridge, MA: Harvard University Press, 1953; revised edition 1961).

12. Dan R. Stiver, "Theological Method," *The Cambridge Companion to Postmodern Theology*, ed. Kevin J. Vanhoozer (New York: Cambridge University Press, 2003), 173.

13. Steven Best and Douglas Kellner, *The Postmodern Adventure* (New York: Guilford Press, 2001), 26.

14. John Caputo, *Deconstruction in a Nutshell* (New York: Fordham University Press, 1997), 59.

15. See Edward O. Wilson, *Consilience: The Unity of Knowledge* (New York: Vintage, 1999).

16. Best and Kellner, 31.

17. Trevor Hart, *Faith Thinking: The Dynamics of Christian Theology* (Downers Grove, IL: InterVarsity, 1995), 21.

CHAPTER 6

1. Keep in mind that the church fathers were rather important for the Reformers and that Luther read quite a bit of Augustine, among many other church fathers. However, in the wake of the Reformation and the shift to the modern age, many Christians began to rely less and less on the interpretations of the past.

2. A literal reading of Revelation has been popularized through the LEFT BEHIND series, and the book of Isaiah is a prophetic book that touches on historical events and makes some predictions about the future. Christians can make some huge mistakes when they take a prophetic book and begin to claim that certain parts of it are being fulfilled today. One fairly innocuous example is a group of Christians in America who read about a highway of holiness in Isaiah 35, and concluded that this must refer to Interstate 35. Though they didn't harm anyone with this interpretation, they certainly seem to have missed the point of Isaiah 35.

3. Nancey Murphy, *Beyond Liberalism and Fundamentalism* (Harrisburg, PA: Trinity Press International, 1996), 2.

4. I can sense that your pulse might be quickening now. Is the Bible completely inerrant? To be honest, I can't say for sure.

It depends what you mean by "inerrant." But we need to ask ourselves why this is so important. I think most Christians can agree that the Bible is true, reliable, trustworthy, and accurate. Is it possible that the literary conventions of the times allowed writers to change some minor details in a story or in a story's chronology if it suited the author's purpose? Perhaps. This doesn't mean they were being deceptive, only that they were theologians who were not primarily reporting facts, but teaching theological lessons. The facts remain true and reliable, but telling a blow-by-blow account like a contemporary historian wasn't the biblical writers' main priority.

5. Spencer Burke (*Heretic's Guide to Eternity* [San Francisco: Jossey-Bass, 2006]) and Brian McLaren (*The Last Word and the Word After That* [San Francisco: Jossey-Bass, 2003]), for example, are two contextual theologians and pastors who have come under fire for questioning the traditional view on hell. While I don't necessarily agree with them, I think they at least bring up issues that call for careful thought and discussion. All the same, some still have doubts about the merit of their views. For an example of a thoughtful critique of Burke's writing, see Scott McKnight's post http://www.jesuscreed.org/?p=1319.

6. Actually, a fourth response to culture exists: Assimilation. Some liberal churches in the modern age took this approach as they readily adopted the modern understanding of the world and simply reshaped their Christian faith accordingly. While some might think this works for the postmodern age, this approach is too problematic to even consider here.

7. Examples of these Christians include fundamentalists and some other conservative Christians. Some could argue that Catholics fall into this camp as well, but I personally find it hard to distinguish between the generally progressive and culturally

relevant theology of Catholic theologians and the practice of mass and numerous beliefs that surely resulted more from the values of a particular culture rather than the revelation of God (two examples include the Catholic teachings on contraception and the requirement that priests and nuns not marry).

8. Craig Van Gelder, "Missional Context: Understanding North American Culture," *Missional Church: A Vision for the Sending of the Church in North America*, ed. Darrell Guder (Grand Rapids: Eerdmans, 1998), 8.

9. Many conservative evangelicals fall into this category, especially seeker-sensitive churches. For example, many Presbyterian (PCA) congregations hold to their traditional theology yet engage in wonderful ministry in their communities. In fact, I've found PCA churches among the most innovative when it comes to rethinking ministry practices in today's culture.

10. Two books that do a good job of bringing together a diverse group of Christians are *The Cambridge Companion to Evangelical Theology* (Cambridge, England: Cambridge University Press, 2007) and *An Emergent Manifesto of Hope* (Grand Rapids, MI: Baker, 2007).

11. Christians in this camp include house churches (www.ptmin .org), the emerging church (www.emergentvillage.com and http://tallskinnykiwi.typepad.com/emergant/), missional communities (www.friendofmissional.org/), scattered renewal groups among traditional denominations such as the Episcopal and Anglican Churches (http://submerge.typepad.com, maggidawn.typepad.com), some neo-orthodox theologians (http://findarticles.com/p/articles/mi_qa3664/is_200004/ ai_n8882455), and some liberal/mainline congregations (http:// pomomusings.com/ and www.emergentvillage.com/weblog/ mainline-emergents-update-from-troy-bronsink). There are

Christians dialoguing with culture from just about every large denomination and from most theological backgrounds.

CHAPTER 7

2. Stanley Grenz, *Renewing the Center: Evangelical Theology in a Post-Theological Era* (Grand Rapids: Baker, 2000), 206–207.

3. Merold Westphal, *Overcoming Ontotheology* (New York: Fordham University Press, 2001), 87.

4. J. R. Briggs, a friend of mine who leads a Christian community, has found lectio divina helpful. See http://brokenstainedglass .typepad.com/broken_stained_glass/2006/11/lectio_divina .html.

5. Thomas Keating, *The Classical Monastic Practice of Lectio Divina*, http://www.centeringprayer.com/lectio/lectio.htm. See also *The Cloud of Unknowing* (Mahwah, NJ: Paulist Press, 1981).

6. Jeanne Guyon, *Experiencing the Depths of Jesus Christ* (Beaumont: Seed Sowers, 1975), 5.

7. Guyon, 8.

8. Scot McKnight has also written an excellent book about prayer called *Praying with the Church* (Brewster, MA: Paraclete Press, 2006).

CHAPTER 8

1. Susanna Clarke, *Jonathan Strange and Mr. Norrell* (New York: Bloomsbury, 2004).

2. Agnostic theologian Bart Ehrman claims the Bible was drastically changed and modified by its keepers and translators throughout history in his book *Misquoting Jesus:*

The Story Behind Who Changed the Bible and Why (New York: HarperCollins, 2005). Ehrman, a former Christian, was previously a conservative believer who held to the complete inerrancy of the Bible but was deeply unsettled by the sloppy collection of manuscripts he found when studying our sources for the Bible. Any student of Greek or Hebrew knows that the Bible is a patchwork of manuscripts, some older and more reliable than others, but Ehrman's questioning of the Bible's reliability and truthfulness goes too far. Even if all of his allegations against scribes for manuscript and translation error are correct (and I don't believe they are), there's no reason to throw out a generally trustworthy and reliable book simply because it doesn't live up to our modern standards in several areas. See the response to Ehrman by Timothy Paul Jones: *Misquoting Truth: A Guide to the Fallacies of Bart Ehrman's* Misquoting Jesus (Downers Grove, IL: InterVarsity, 2007).

3. Dan R. Stiver, "Theological Method," *The Cambridge Companion to Postmodern Theology*, ed. Kevin J. Vanhoozer (New York: Cambridge University Press, 2003), 181.

4. This is called the historical-critical method of interpreting Scripture. The aim is to study Scripture within the cultural, literary, and historical context of the original books, attempting to discern the author's intention and how it would have been read by the original audience. This is a standard interpretive method for many Christians. Keep in mind that anything I suggest adding to this method doesn't amount to an abandonment of this method.

5. Paul obviously isn't saying that the law in and of itself is evil; in 2 Timothy 3:16, Paul states that all Scripture is profitable in some way.

6. Kevin J. Vanhoozer, "Scripture and Tradition," *Cambridge*

Companion to Postmodern Theology, ed. Kevin J. Vanhoozer (New York: Cambridge University Press, 2003), 165.

7. Stanley Grenz, "Ecclesiology," *Cambridge Companion to Postmodern Theology*, ed. Kevin J. Vanhoozer (New York: Cambridge University Press, 2003), 262.

8. Lesslie Newbigin, *The Gospel in a Pluralist Society* (Grand Rapids: Eerdmans, 1989), 95.

9. John Franke and Stanley Grenz, *Beyond Foundationalism: Shaping Theology in a Postmodern Context* (Louisville, KY: Westminster John Knox Press, 2001), 67.

10. Trevor Hart, *Faith Thinking: The Dynamics of Christian Theology* (Downers Grove, IL: InterVarsity, 1995), 11.

11. Vanhoozer, "Scripture and Tradition," *Cambridge Companion to Postmodern Theology*, 161.

12. For a balanced discussion of this issue, see James R. Beck and Craig Blomberg, *Two Views on Women in Ministry* (Grand Rapids, MI: Zondervan, 2001).

13. "The TNIV Debate," *Christianity Today*, October 7, 2002, http://www.christianitytoday.com/ct/2002/october7/1.36.html.

14. TNIV Truth, http://tnivtruth.blogspot.com/.

15. When trying to evaluate a translation, read the principles of translation in the front of the Bible. This brief introduction to the methods used by the translators can help you understand what kind of translation you hold.

16. Of course, no student of the Bible should use the NLT or *The Message* alone, but they are essential tools when used as one part of a more comprehensive study of Scripture.

17. The casual visitor to a used bookstore or library book sale might find copies of Donald Barclay's popular commentary DAILY BIBLE STUDY SERIES (Westminster: John Knox Press). While these are surely helpful resources, my opinion is that this series

hardly holds a candle to the works by theologians such as N. T. Wright.

18. Christian Apologetics and Research Ministry, "The Jehovah's Witnesses and John 1:1," http://www.carm.org/jw/john1_1.htm.

19. See Cole's excellent book *Organic Church: Growing Faith Where Life Happens* (San Francisco: Jossey-Bass, 2005) for the ways he ties together Bible study with organic church planting.

CHAPTER 9

1. Tony Jones, "More on Wheaton," Theoblogy, April 24, 2007, http://theoblogy.blogspot.com/2007/04/more-on-wheaton.html.

2. Catholics believe that tradition and Scripture are uniquely intertwined because the church selected which books to include in the Bible. This is a sensible way to view the matter, but I still take the Protestant view of the issue because the Scriptures themselves are a far more stable and reliable source of theology than the changing views of the church over time. For a more thorough treatment of this issue, see Roger Olson's *The Mosaic of Christian Belief: Twenty Centuries of Unity and Diversity* (Downers Grove, IL: InterVarsity, 2002), 99–101.

3. Olson, 54.

4. Olson, 57.

5. For more about Constantine and the Christian church of the early fourth century see Gonzalez, Justo L. *The Story of Christianity: Complete in One Volume The Early Church to the Present Day.* (Peabody: Prince Press, 2007), 102-167.

6. John Franke and Stanley Grenz, *Beyond Foundationalism: Shaping Theology in a Postmodern Context* (Louisville, KY: Westminster John Knox Press, 2001), 124.

7. Kevin J. Vanhoozer, "Scripture and Tradition," *The Cambridge Companion to Postmodern Theology*, ed. Kevin J. Vanhoozer

(New York: Cambridge University Press, 2003), 153.

8. Franke and Grenz, *Beyond Foundationalism*, 24.

9. Dan R. Stiver, "Theological Method," *The Cambridge Companion to Postmodern Theology*, 182.

10. Olson, 63.

11. Franke and Grenz, *Beyond Foundationalism*, 124.

12. The Essene community at Qumran is just one of many Essene communities from that time, but thanks to the Dead Sea Scrolls and the findings of archaeologists, they are the most famous.

13. See the Commentary on Nahum, 4Q169 from *The Complete Dead Sea Scrolls in English*, trans. Geza Vermes. (New York: Penguin Books, 1998), 473–477. For a comprehensive and extremely helpful study of the Jewish literature between the testaments and its relevance for biblical study, see Larry Helyer's *Exploring Jewish Literature of the Second Temple Period*, (Downers Grove, IL: InterVarsity, 2002). As his research assistant for this project, I can personally affirm Helyer's rigorous scholarship and accessible style that make this book a tremendous gift for Christians today.

14. There are a variety of traditions related to purgatory that church fathers held before Thomas Aquinas formulated the doctrine of purgatory that we generally know of today.

15. "Arminianism is a theological tradition based upon the teachings of the sixteenth-century Dutch Protestant theologian Jacobus Arminius and later developed by the eighteenth-century English evangelist John Wesley, which affirms human free will and denies predestination." (Ted Dorman, *A Faith for All Seasons: Historic Christian Belief in Its Classical Expression* (Nashville: Broadman and Holman, 1995), 370.

CHAPTER 10

1. *Intifada* refers to an "uprising" or "shaking off." Palestinians apply this to their opposition to the Israeli occupation of the lands they believe to be their own.

2. I don't believe this today. Both parties share the blame, not to mention the United Nations. The Israeli War for Independence arose out of events reaching back to the beginning of the 1900s, so to place the blame squarely on one party and not the other is naive.

3. *Wikipedia*, citing the U.S. Central Intelligence Agency, states that Hutus comprise 84–85 percent of Burundi and Rwandan population, making them the largest of the two nations' three ethnic groups, vastly outstripping the next largest group, the Tutsis, against whom radical Hutus perpetrated the Rwandan genocide of 1994. Though cited as ethnic, the division between the two groups is more one of social class, as they are linguistically, culturally, and genetically similar, especially when compared to the third group, the Twa pygmies, who, though they share the language and culture of the majority of the population, exhibit recognized genetic differences (Wikipedia contributors, "Hutu," *Wikipedia: The Free Encyclopedia*, http://en.wikipedia.org/wiki/Hutu).

4. BBC News, "Rwanda Priest Tried for Genocide," September 20, 2004, http://news.bbc.co.uk/1/hi/world/africa/3671464 .stm. See also Jason Beaubien, "Catholic Complicity and Rwanda Genocide," *National Public Radio*, April 22, 2005, http://www.npr.org/templates/story/story.php?storyId=4615171.

5. Emily Wax, "Islam Attracting Many Survivors of Rwanda Genocide," *The Washington Post*, September 23, 2002, http://www.washingtonpost.com/wp-dyn/articles/A53018- 2002Sep22.html.

6. Scot McKnight, "The Big 'You' and the Bible, Part 1," March 19, 2007, http://www.jesuscreed.org/?p=2154.

7. There is a lot of literature out there on this topic. One good place to start is James R. Beck and Craig Blomberg, eds., *Two Views on Women in Ministry* (Grand Rapids, MI: Zondervan, 2001).

8. Ray S. Anderson, *An Emergent Theology for Emerging Churches* (Downers Grove, IL: InterVarsity, 2006), 41.

9. C. Rene Padilla, "Evangelical Theology in Latin America," *The Cambridge Companion to Evangelical Theology*, eds. Timothy Larsen and Daniel J. Treier (Cambridge: Cambridge University Press, 2007), 264.

10. Padilla, 270.

11. Robert Webber, *The Younger Evangelicals: Facing the Challenges of the New World* (Grand Rapids, MI: Baker, 2002), 101.

12. Webber, 65.

CHAPTER 11

1. While some Christians can abuse the gifts of the Spirit, I believe the Toronto Blessing was a genuine move of the Holy Spirit. I've experienced similar events in person and found nothing unbiblical about them. In addition, a review of revivals throughout history reveals similar manifestations, particularly intense weeping or intense laughter. I personally advocate caution when tempted to criticize something that may be the work of the Holy Spirit, for Jesus said "anyone who speaks against the Holy Spirit will not be forgiven, either in this age or in the age to come" (Matthew 12:32).

2. For more about Hanegraaff's views, see his book *Counterfeit Revival: Looking for God in All the Wrong Places* (Nashville: Thomas Nelson, 2001).

3. I mean to say that these things were completely foreign to me and while not wrong, were very outside of my orderly Christian tradition.
4. I don't have space here to do his presentation justice, but the confusion generally arises from the translation of the Latin word for "merit."
5. I am indebted to Roger Olson and Stanley Grenz for this term. See Olson's book *The Mosaic of Christian Beliefs: Twenty Centuries of Unity and Diversity* (Downers Grove, IL: InterVarsity, 2002).

ABOUT THE AUTHOR

ED CYZEWSKI (MDiv Biblical Theological Seminary) works in the nonprofit sector of southwest Vermont and as a freelance writer. He has served as the chair and communications chair of the Northshire Nonprofit Network, a group of nonprofits committed to nonprofit collaboration, education, and advocacy. He serves with several ministries and nonprofit organizations in Vermont and volunteers with Shevet Achim, a Christian organization committed to helping non-Israeli children receive life saving medical care in Israel. He blogs regularly on theology at http://inamirrordimly.com and on writing at www.edcyz.com.

WWW.NOTFORSALECAMPAIGN.ORG

Not for Sale is a campaign of students, entrepreneurs, artists, people of faith, athletes, law enforcement officers, politicians, social workers, skilled professionals, and all justice seekers, united to fight the global slave trade.

Not for Sale aims to educate and mobilize an international abolitionist movement through the innovation and implementation of open-source activism. Inside the United States, the campaign identifies trafficking rings and collaborates with local law enforcement and community groups to shut them down and provide support for the victims. Internationally, the campaign partners with poorly resourced abolitionist groups to enhance their capacity.

Every single person has a skill that they can give
to free an individual living in bondage.

Other Great Titles by NavPress on Theology in the Postmodern Era!

The God Who Smokes
Timothy J. Stoner
ISBN-13: 978-1-60006-247-6
ISBN-10: 1-60006-247-4

Perhaps no recent spiritual movement has caused more division than the emergent church. With a casual, narrative voice, Timothy Stoner presents an unwavering answer to the postmodern cry for an authentic, knowable truth that is compassionate and courageous demonstrated in sacrificial commitment to a life of righteousness and justice.

Free to Be Bound
Jonathan Wilson-Hartgrove
ISBN-13: 978-1-60006-190-5
ISBN-10: 1-60006-190-7

We have become so immune to the division that we don't notice it infecting the church. Jonathan Wilson-Hartgrove realizes the need for black and white Christians to become united in a new way and proposes a fresh vision of Christian identity beyond the confines of race.

How Can a Good God Let Bad Things Happen?
Mark Tabb
ISBN-13: 978-1-60006-268-1
ISBN-10: 1-60006-268-7

In a world where tragedy and catastrophe strike daily, God's people pray for blessings but feel abandoned. Author Mark Tabb takes readers through the story of Job to show that God has not forsaken us.

Go Deeper into Postmodernism Issues with the Bible Study and Discussion Guide!

Coffeehouse Theology Bible Study

Ed Cyzewski
ISBN-13: 978-1-60006-278-0
ISBN-10: 1-60006-278-4

A relationship with God is central to life-breathing theology, but today's culture experiences a barrier of ignorance and misunderstanding of the Church's mission. Go deeper into the issues of postmodernism with Ed's companion bible study to *Coffeehouse Theology*.

Coffeehouse Theology Discussion Guide

Ed Cyzewski
ISBN-13: 978-1-60006-299-5
ISBN-10: 1-60006-299-7

Christian readers will find a conversational guide to theology in the postmodernism context and in the emerging church, helping them understand, shape, and live out practical Christian theology.

The Message//Remix: SOLO

ISBN-13: 978-1-60006-105-9
ISBN-10: 1-60006-105-2

In *Coffeehouse Theology*, Ed references The Message//Remix: SOLO, and innovative devotional designed to change how you interact with God's Word. *The Message Remix: Solo* revolves around lectio divina, or "divine reading," an ancient approach to exploring Scripture.